ix

Foam Sandwich Boatbuilding

Foam Sandwich Boatbuilding

A Practical Guide to Home Construction

by Peter Wynn

With an Introduction by Derek Kelsall

London · George Allen & Unwin Ltd
Ruskin House   Museum Street

First published in 1972

ISBN 0 04 623010 6

Printed in Great Britain
in 11 point Times Roman type
by Unwin Brothers Limited
Woking and London

Introduction

To build one's own boat is a most satisfying achievement. You watch it take shape due to your own efforts and then launch it into its natural element. However, before you reach the launching date there will have been many hours of hard work spent, and some hours of frustration; there will be a few moments of elation as particular stages are reached, but most of it will have been quite hard work, and many aspiring builders give up along the way. Hence it is very important that the method of building is chosen with great care, in the light of one's capability and experience.

Glass fibre, because it is a very strong and durable material, is used to build some 80 per cent of small boats produced today. Professional boat builders have long recognized its advantages over more traditional materials but the amateur builder has been confined to the less efficient ply or other forms of timber construction. That glass fibre has to be laminated into a mould is a generally accepted limitation of the material and few amateurs can afford to build an expensive mould for one hull only. Just a handful of builders have attempted 'one off' glass fibre methods. Of these *sandwich construction* has proved to be the most successful and this book should be read by every person considering building his own boat.

Yachtsmen are a pretty conservative race by nature so I would like to give a little of the history of sandwich construction which is probably not so recent as most people believe. About fifteen years ago a Dutch yard built two 80-foot pilot cutters using Airex P.V.C. foam and G.R.P. and all types of boats have been built in various parts of the world since, using a similar system. Sandwich construction first attracted my attention about eight years ago and my building experience ranges from a 10-foot dinghy to a 30-ton ketch. I can state categorically that I know of no case of sandwich construction failing. There are a number of outstanding cases where sandwich construction yachts have survived a wrecking that would have 'written off' any other boat. So please do not dismiss sandwich construction as some new-fangled idea that is a passing phase. As long as there are individuals who want 'one off' designs there will be some form of sandwich construction.

Basically the method is very simple and with the guidance offered in this book it is well within the capabilities of the average do-it-yourself handyman. Very little special equipment is needed and this is true whether the boat is to be 10-foot or 50-foot.

If I have not entirely convinced you (the amateur builder) of the value of sandwich construction from the point of view of suitability and simplicity let us have a look at some other aspects of sandwich construction. Durability is the most important property

9

1. The *Sir Thomas Lipton*, sailed by Geoffrey Williams to win the Single-Handed Transatlantic Yacht Race—*Photo: Keystone Press.*

of G.R.P. and requires no elaboration here. A common criticism of solid G.R.P. boats is that they are like bath tubs—cold to the touch and lacking the character and feel of a well-built timber vessel. Sandwich construction goes a long way towards eliminating this. Even $\frac{1}{2}''$ of P.V.C. is a good insulator which considerably reduces the problem of condensation and loses the 'cold-to-the-touch' feeling. Everyone interested in boats must have thumped a small G.R.P. hull and been amazed at how flexible and thin it felt. The reason is that glass fibre is not a stiff material like steel or wood and stiffness can only be achieved in solid G.R.P. by increasing the thickness of the laminate and this means extra weight and cost. This becomes an increasing problem with size. Sandwich construction, however, immediately achieves stiffness due to the thickness of the foam. This is one reason why sandwich construction can be designed lighter in weight than solid G.R.P.

Another reason is that we can use the stronger-woven roving as opposed to C.S.M. which requires less resin and which can therefore save up to 40 per cent of the weight. In engineering some form of sandwich is often applied where strength for minimum weight is required. It can be compared with an I beam where the heavy top and bottom flanges take the tensile and compressive loads and the lighter webb takes the shear stresses.

The average sandwich laminate will be around 80 per cent foam and 20 per cent G.R.P. which means we have a substantial amount of built-in buoyancy. Rigid P.V.C. foam, which is the only core material that I can recommend for this type of building, has almost ideal properties for a core material. It does not absorb water and is unaffected by most chemicals. If the skin is damaged only the immediate area is affected and is easily repaired.

Impact resistance is good due to the resilience of the P.V.C. foam. Where resin and glass is laid directly on to the foam the bond is excellent and again I can state that I know of no case of delamination failure. The weight at 5 pounds per cubic foot, the compression and shear strengths all contribute to making the P.V.C. foam first choice.

The cost of sandwich is high in initial material costs (P.V.C. foam costs approximately the same as plywood for the same thickness), but any complete analysis including such things as insulation, lower power requirements, maintenance, etc., will prove sandwich to be more economical in the long term.

My involvement with sandwich construction is very closely associated with my trimaran designs. Having built plywood trimarans and sailed them for many thousands of miles I had designed my 'ideal trimaran' but it just did not lend itself to conventional construction methods. My search for a suitable method of building revolved round G.R.P. and foam but it was, in fact, a chance meeting in New York that put me on to the use of P.V.C. sandwich. I was given the opportunity to inspect a sandwich construction demountable trimaran and later helped to assemble and sail this vessel which, I believe, was one of the first to be built in the United States with this method. At this time a few vessels had already been built in Europe. However, it was not until the middle of 1965 that I was able to start my own experiments with the material. This led to my first success—a 42-foot trimaran *Toria*—which was a runaway winner in the 1966 Round Britain Race.

The following are some of the sandwich-construction vessels that are worthy of note with some of their accomplishments.

Toria: 42-foot trimaran. Derek Kelsall design. Winner of 1966 Round Britain Race.

Trifle: 42-foot trimaran. Derek Kelsall design. Fastest multihull in the United Kingdom.

Sir Thomas Lipton: 57-foot ketch. R. Clark design. Winner of 1968 Single-Handed Trans Atlantic Race.

Trumpeter: 44-foot trimaran. Derek Kelsall Design. Third in 1970 Round Britain Race; first in 1971 Bermuda Race.

They are four very different but successful boats that I would like to believe owe some of their success to their common method of construction—P.V.C. foam sandwich.

We have built all types of boat since *Toria* but the method has remained basically unchanged. Naturally, many of the practical details of producing the boats have been changed and improved from the point of view of cost, quality, and strength. For example for *Toria's* first hull we used a needle and string to attach the foam to the former. This worked satisfactorily but removing the hull involved cutting thousands of string loops which left the inside of the hull looking like a blow up of an unshaven chin. Each 'hair' had to be tediously cut back right against the foam before the inside skin could be applied.

When you reach the end of this book I am confident that you will say it all sounds quite simple and straightforward. Careful and conscientious work is required to achieve the best results, but these are qualities that the amateur can provide without effort.

As I say to all amateur builders do not underestimate the amount of time and very hard work involved in boat-building, but having decided to build you will be best off with glass fibre and P.V.C. foam sandwich construction. It is easier than you think, and with this simple-to-understand book as a guide there are few pitfalls that you are likely to meet.

Derek Kelsall

Contents

Illustrations

PLATES

FIGURES

Preface

Before I get down to the details of how to build a foam sandwich boat let me tell you something about myself and how I came to write this book.

When we built our boat I was thirty-four years old and a design student studying pottery at an art college in England (due to one thing and another I started my education a bit later than most people). Pamela, my wife, teaches infants at the local school and we have a son of five called Guy.

For several years, since we got married in fact, we lived in a normal sort of semi-detached in a normal sort of London suburb. Weekends and summer holidays we spent in a small cruising catamaran bouncing from one mud bank to the next on the east coast, never going out of sight of land, in fact rarely ever leaving contact with it. Then around Christmas 1969 we decided it was time we had a change. Somehow, though neither of us had ever been to sea, we decided we wanted to live on a boat. We liked the space and stability of catamarans, so it had to be a catamaran. We put the house on the market and did some arithmetic. Like most people we found we needed ten times as much money as we actually had to do what we wanted. The sort of boat we could afford in hull form or second hand just was not big enough for a full-time living proposition—so we looked at the possibilities of building one ourselves.

Steel, ferro-cement, the various methods of construction in wood, all came under close scrutiny. As far as I could see all of them called for precision, skills and tenacity to greater extents than I could boast. Skills I could probably learn, but I am just not the sort of person to slog away, week after week, possibly for three or four years at the same task. And this is what I would have to expect if we attempted to build using any of these methods.

That really was a rather worrying time. Then, quite by chance, a friend from the sailing club mentioned that there was going to be an Amateur Yacht Research Society meeting the following week on yacht construction and that Derek Kelsall was going to talk about foam sandwich, was I interested? At this stage of course our plans for building a boat were a dark secret between Pamela and myself, though the estate agents knew about selling the house.

I had read the literature available on how *Toria* was built and had decided that this idea of heating the sheets of foam, in the sort of polythene shelter I envisaged us working in, was not really on. But perhaps Derek Kelsall would tell us more about it at the meeting. Not only did he tell us more, he introduced us to Airex foam which does not need heat to make it bend. John Beswick was also at the meeting: an amateur,

2. *Jollywitch*—her last moment on land.

he had just built a 42-foot trimaran called *Leen Valley Venturer*, in foam sandwich (he later sailed her in the Round Britain Race), and according to him it really was as simple as it sounded. A brief visit to Sandwich Marina the following week to see the method actually in operation and I was convinced that here was a way of building a boat that was suitable for me. Some more arithmetic and we decided that, even allowing for unforeseen expenses, we would be able to afford a 40-foot catamaran. We would not be able to rig it and fit it out completely at first, but this did not seem terribly important when we considered the size of boat we were getting, and so far I have found no reason to change that opinion.

We decided to write this book because there is a total lack of detailed, practical information on this form of construction.

We wasted an awful lot of time, and a fair amount of money, because we had to find out for ourselves how to do things as we went along. Derek Kelsall was a great help, but he was in Kent, we were in Essex and telephone calls are expensive.

I am sure more amateurs will start building in foam sandwich as its advantages are realized and this bogey is laid about amateurs using resin under less-than-ideal conditions. I hope this book will help others to avoid the mistakes we made and to do things even more quickly and easily than we did. As an amateur I faced the problems that any other amateur will face, and from this point of view I probably know more than most experts; I do not know so much that I have forgotten what it is like to know nothing at all.

I have tried to be as detailed and explicit as possible throughout the book, not because the method of construction is complicated but for the benefit of people, like myself a year ago, who know next to nothing about resinglass and have only a sketchy grasp of boatbuilding techniques generally. Many people I am sure will find they can skip through the text, look at the pictures and get all the information they need to build a foam sandwich boat.

Where I know of alternative methods or materials I have mentioned them but mainly this is an account of the methods and materials we found effective, which on the whole are the same as those employed by Derek Kelsall at Sandwich Marina.

At the back of the book I have listed the materials and equipment that are necessary for building in foam sandwich. This is intended as a ready reference section primarily for costing and ordering purposes and should ensure that nothing gets overlooked, only to rear its expensive head at a later date.

Since building our boat I have met one or two 'experts' who at the mention of foam sandwich nod their head knowingly and say vaguely, 'There are snags, delamination, poor impact strength, and other things you know.' When I have tried to pin them down to actual cases they have all looked embarrassed and muttered something about, 'not being able to say any more at the moment'. The first time it happened I was terribly worried. Now I equate such remarks with similar ones made in the early days of glass fibre, and simply remind myself that many foam-sandwich boats, like the *Sir Thomas*

20

Lipton and even the amateur-built *Leen Valley Venturer*, have successfully withstood harder conditions for far longer than any boat I build is going to have to withstand.

Another point to bear in mind is that, for all the advances of technology, boat building is still an art rather than a science, and what is $\frac{1}{4}''$ in thirty feet?

Now, at the time of writing, the launching date for our boat has been fixed and we are in the middle of the last minute panic to get as many loose ends tied-up as possible. We have already started on the fitting-out and it promises to be as rewarding as the building of the shell.

All in all it has been quite a year; a little blood and tears; one or two laughs; a lot of sweat and toil; but above all a wonderful feeling of achievement and quiet satisfaction.

3. *Leen Valley Venturer*, built by John Beswick in his garage, almost unaided, is one of the first entirely amateur-constructed foam sandwich craft—*Photo: John Beswick*.

4. Our 40-foot catamaran as she was after sixteen hundred hours work, when winter set in. In front is the mould for the hulls.

The Method

The sandwich of a foam sandwich boat is made from a layer of light, almost rigid plastic foam, between skins of glass-reinforced plastic.

To form the shape a simple wooden mould like that in Plate 4 is made, over which the foam is bent. Resinglass is then applied to the outside. When this has cured the shell is lifted off and resinglass put on the inside.

A simple wooden support for the decks is then built into the hull. The decks are cut and resinglassed on one side flat on the ground before being put permanently into place on the hull. Once in place the outside of the foam is resinglassed.

The whole process is just about as simple as it sounds, and very nearly as quick.

P.V.C. foam/G.R.P. sandwich is so versatile it can be used to make just about any sort of craft—sail or power, mono-hull or multi-hull. The properties inherent in the method of construction however lend themselves more to some types of design than to others. To start with foam sandwich is a light form of construction, so it lends itself to light-displacement sailing vessels and planing-power craft, rather than to the heavy weights which are designed for ferro-cement construction.

Because it is easy to form over curved surfaces there is no reason to build a hard chine craft unless the chine has some specific design function, as in the after-bodies of high-speed power craft and some dinghies.

Anyone contemplating either designing specifically for foam sandwich construction or modifying an existing design for this method would do well to consult Derek Kelsall, or another naval architect with foam sandwich experience to make sure that the contemplated design is suitable, and also to get the necessary structural details drawn up by a professional.

Derek Kelsall in his Foreword has remarked that foam sandwich is an expensive method of building a boat. And so it is. But unlike other methods of building it does not look cheap to start with and then turn out otherwise. In fact when you take into account the cost of all the internal stiffening and fastenings needed with most other forms of construction I am not at all sure that foam sandwich is that much more expensive, and it certainly seems to be a lot quicker and easier than other methods.

At 1970 prices, with resin at 9p a pound, woven roving at 28p a pound, and 12mm. Airex foam at 22p a square foot, the material cost for our 40-foot catamaran shell was £1,500.

Physical strength is rarely required when making a sandwich craft as it is constructed layer by layer from small batches of materials. And provided you think that your relationship is strong enough to stand the strain there is no reason why a wife should not take as much part as her husband in the building process.

Although resinglass calls for careful, conscientious work, precise cutting and bending are not required. In fact it is easiest if everything is cut slightly on the small side and any gaps filled with slithers of foam and resin putty.

The mould is probably the most daunting thing about a sandwich boat. We even went to the trouble of getting a couple of quotes from professional yards for the job. In the event it turned out that its manufacture was one of the pleasantest jobs of the summer.

Because the mould stringers can be packed up if necessary to fair up the mould even the frames used in making the mould need not be very accurately cut. There is no need to carry out a full-size lofting operation. It is quite sufficient to draw the frames full size using the designer's table of offsets.

Resinglass work must be done carefully to get the maximum strength from the material, and precautions must be taken to stop water in any form from coming into contact with fresh resin work. But otherwise we found no problems in using the materials even though we had no previous experience with them.

It is possible that an amateur built foam sandwich boat will not be quite as symmetrical and as well finished as the professional job. And it will almost certainly be heavier because amateurs tend to increase the sizes of fitting and to add extra pieces of unnecessary resinglass all over the place (I have to plead guilty I am afraid). It is, however, extremely unlikely that an amateur will ever make a leaky or unsafe foam sandwich boat (provided the design is good).

Leaks in a foam sandwich craft are very rare. There are virtually two boats, one inside the other, and both of them are made from resinglass, which, for all practical purposes, can be considered impervious to water.

The Mould

To make the mould timber frames corresponding to the sections of the boat are set up on a timber support or strong back. Wooden stringers are then screwed on fore and aft over the frames. Finally the mould is faired up by packing up or paring down the stringers where necessary.

The mould to a large extent determines how true or otherwise the finished hull is going to be so it pays to spend a fair amount of time getting things reasonably right. The mould for the hulls of our 40′ catamaran took 150 hours to build, while that for the dinghy in the photographs some 20 hours. Within reason none of the timber sizes are critical and our mould was constructed almost entirely from second-hand timber bought from demolition contractors.

None of the timber need be planed, though the timber used for stringers should be of reasonably constant thickness. The easiest way to ensure this is to run it through a thicknesser, if you have access to one, but we used ordinary sawn timber direct from the wood yard and experienced no difficulty in fairing up the mould. Using sawn rather than finished timber meant we picked up quite a lot of small splinters, but they were never any problem.

The strong back for the mould is made from $8'' \times 2''$ timber. We found second-hand $9'' \times 2''$ joists cheaper than new $8'' \times 2''$ ones, so we used them.

The frames can be cut from $6'' \times 1''$ though we found $6'' \times \frac{3}{4}''$ second-hand floor boards cheaper and quite adequate. One inch by one inch is ideal for the stringers. We in fact used $1\frac{1}{2}'' \times \frac{3}{4}''$, which was just about thick enough for a span of $39''$ between the frames. Had the gap been wider, it would not have been stiff enough.

Some $2'' \times 1''$ is needed for bracing the frames and making centre lines down each frame (Fig. 1). Before the frames can be cut the thickness of the stringers has to be known, and suppliers being what they are undoubtedly the best thing is to have your stringer material delivered and then measure the thickness yourself. Once you know the thickness of the stringers, foam, and resinglass lay-up which you are going to use, you can start on the frames.

First draw up the half-sections full size. The easiest way is to plot from the table of offsets on to a large piece of paper or on to a piece of painted hardboard. You should end up with something like the section part of the lines drawing, only at full size, sections 1–5 on one side of the centre line, 6–10 on the other.

Then add up the thickness of your stringers and foam, plus a little for the outer glass skin, allow about $\frac{3}{32}''$ for two layers of 18 oz. undirectional woven roving and a little filler. In our case this was $\frac{3}{4}''$ for the stringers, $\frac{1}{2}''$ for the foam and $\frac{3}{32}''$ for the resinglass, making $1\frac{11}{32}''$ total.

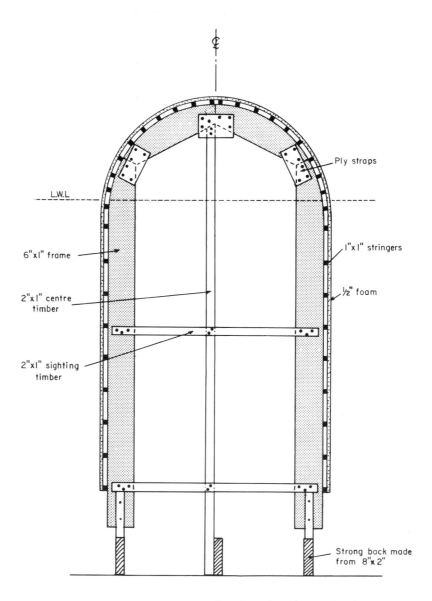

Fig. 1. Typical section through a catamaran hull and mould. The outside line of resinglass is that shown on the line drawing. It is clear from this that allowance has to be made for the thickness of the foam and the stringers before the frames are cut.

The full-size sections less this amount give the shape and size of the mould frames. If you have drawn your sections on hardboard step in the required amount with dividers or a pair of compasses (the cheaper friction sort are better for this job than expensive spring bow ones), and draw a new set of lines in a different-coloured pencil or pen. If you have drawn your sections on paper, tape this to a piece of hardboard and then prick through, again with dividers or compasses, to the frame size. The prick marks can now be joined up, either freehand or with the aid of a batten. This way you have one set of lines only on the paper and one set (the frame-size set) on the hardboard, the possibility of confusion is therefore lessened. Remember to prick through the L.W.L. and the centre line.

The measurement for stringers, foam and resinglass has to be subtracted at right angles to the line of the hull, not perpendicular to the centre line, so it is not possible simply to subtract the required amount from each offset in the table and draw the resulting curve.

5. The lines for our 8½-foot dinghy on hardboard with the mould frame size lines drawn inside. The masking tape with nails is ready in position for marking the largest frame.

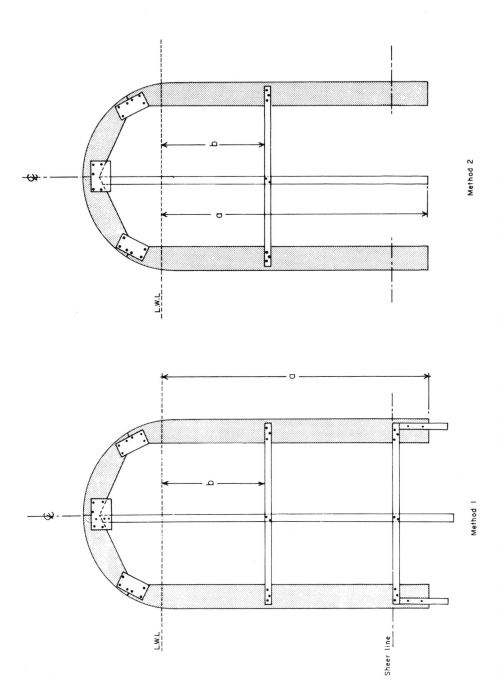

Fig. 2 Typical frames for a catamaran mould. Frames for a mono-hull would be made in exactly the same way. Lengths 'a' and 'b' must be the same on all ten frames.

Later I shall describe two methods for making your strong back and setting up the frames. The frames are basically the same for both methods (Fig. 2) so I shall deal with them together mentioning the variations where they occur.

It helps when setting up if the frames are all made to a common base line a few inches higher (or rather lower because you are working upside down) than the highest point on the sheer line (Fig. 2). It is also necessary to have a perpendicular centre line and a horizontal line on each frame so that they can be lined up. This horizontal must of course be common to all frames and it is best positioned about one third of the way up from the sheer towards the keel on the largest frame. One of the water lines on the lines drawing can be used, or a quite arbitrary line ruled in, it makes no difference. In fact, provided it is the same on all the frames, it does not even have to be at right angles to the centre line, though if it is so much the better.

Starting with station number 5 or 6, lay two pieces of 6″ × 1″ on your drawing so that all the frame is covered but the minimum of timber is wasted—this will normally put the joint at the turn of the bilges. Mark the mitre where the pieces join and cut. Relay the two pieces, which should now lie flat on the hardboard, checking that the whole of the frame is in fact covered. Move the pieces about a little if necessary, then mark and cut the other ends. One end will be the centre line of the keel, the other will be beyond the sheer line on an arbitrary line but to which all the frames will be taken.

Remember that you will have to get in and out of the mould to screw on the foam, so make sure that there is enough room between the sheer line and the top of the strong back at some point for you to do this. If your sheer line is particularly straight you may have to extend each frame by sixteen or eighteen inches; a ruler on the lines drawing will tell you how much clearance you have. If you try squeezing yourself under a broom propped across some books or tins you will get some idea of the clearance you need. Tend to be generous rather than otherwise, you will have to go in and out of there quite a lot.

One-inch nails, or rather their heads, offer a simple but remarkably effective way of transferring your lines from the hardboard to the frame timber.

Lay out about four feet of 1″ wide masking tape sticky side up; (you will need a supply of this later for the glassing, so you may as well buy it early and get the bulk price). On this place 1″ round wire nails about an inch apart so that their heads are just off the tape. Put another piece of tape on top so that the two sticky surfaces are together.

Make enough of this tape to go from the keel round to the sheer on your biggest frame. Now lay the tape on the inside of the line you are working to, with the heads of the nails, on the line; go along with a hammer and gently knock each nail so that the head cuts into the hardboard. Place the prepared pieces of 6″ × 1″ in the correct position over the nails, i.e. so that the ends are in the right place at the centre and sheer lines. Then, standing on the wood so that it can not move, give it a sharp clout every six inches or so with a mallet. Lift off the pieces of 6″ × 1″ and no doubt like me you

6. The pieces of 6″ × 1″ for the largest frame ready to have the mallet used on them. The timber should completely cover the nail heads, though it would be possible to pack out the stringers later if the frame was cut as it is in this photograph.

will be amazed and gratified to see a nice fair curve of little dents where the heads of the nails have gone into the wood.

It is a simple matter to join the marks up freehand with a pencil. Perhaps I should just add that the flatter and firmer the base on which you do this hammering the better, the piece of concrete I used was none too smooth and once or twice when I wielded the mallet rather vigorously I bounced off the piece of wood instead of the wood going down on to the nails.

The quickest way, and certainly the cheapest if you are hiring cutting equipment, is to go through and prepare each frame, or rather half frame, in this way, marking the pieces so you know which is which. Then have a session cutting all the prepared pieces plus another of each to make the complete frames. With a band saw it is a simple matter to tack another piece of timber to the one marked and cut the two together. Using a Lesto-type jig saw (and for what they cost to hire for a day there is no point in not using one if you do not own a band saw) you might find it easier to cut one thickness of wood at a time, marking round the second with a sharp pen knife.

If you do use a jig saw have plenty of spare blades (hire shops supply them on a sale or return basis). They seem to last longer if they are kept cool, so it is a good idea to stop every five feet or so and cool the blade with a drop of water—remembering that the tools are electric, and water could not only harm the motor if it gets inside but could prove lethal to the operator. So just a drop and keep it at the blade end. Also be patient and wait until the blade has completely stopped moving before you take it out of the cut, otherwise it will probably get bent, which is not very good.

If your curves tend to look more like a dog's back legs than the beautiful frames you have seen propped up outside the boat yards, do not despair. It is only soft wood so a smoothing plane will quickly take care of the high spots. Leave the low spots well alone, as the stringers that cross these can be packed out at a later date.

7. The first half of the frame nailed up with a ply strap. All the remaining pieces of 6″ × 1″ have been sawn ready to make the other frames.

8.   The frame complete with centre line and sighting line. On a frame of this size one piece
of $2'' \times 1''$ for both sighting and holding the frame together is sufficient.

I am sure most people will be surprised at how easy it is to follow round a line with
a jig saw if a little care is taken, and just how little finishing work there is to do with a
plane, which is rather a pity because $1''$ or $\frac{3}{4}''$ soft wood is so easy to plane it is almost
enjoyable.

The frames are held together with pieces of $\frac{3}{8}''$ or $\frac{1}{2}''$ scrap ply, I got a bag of offcuts
from the local wood yard for free. Lay out the two pieces that make half a frame on
the full-size drawing, put a piece of ply across the joint, then, standing on the pieces of
frame so they do not move, hammer about five nails through each piece of the frame.
The nails need to be long enough to come right through the ply and frame timber so
they can be clenched over. Lay the pieces of timber for the other half of the frame on
top of the half already made and join these with a ply strap. Put the ply strap on the
correct side of this second half so that when the full frame is laid out the two ply straps
are on top.

Lay out the full frame on the full-size drawing. If the two halves meet at the keel line and the other ends come to the base line the same distance each side of the centre line, you should have a symmetrical frame.

Join the two halves with another ply strap at the keel, making this strap overlap the frame timber on the inside of the frame so that you have something to nail the centre line 2″ × 1″ to.

While the frame is still in position on the drawing, nail a piece of 2″ × 1″ across the frame for your sighting line. This needs to be done fairly accurately so use a try square to make sure you are exactly on the line. Another piece of 2″ × 1″ nailed across near the sheer end of the frame will make the job more rigid and prevent the ends of the frame from waving about, though this is only really necessary if you are using the first method for lining up your frames on the strong back.

Slide another piece of 2″ × 1″ under your sighting pieces and the ply strap at the keel, positioning it so that one edge lies on the centre line. Nail it into place. This centre piece needs to extend six inches beyond the base line, or be an inch or two shorter, depending on which method you use to set up your frames. If you use the first method to set up your frames, the length of the centre piece can vary from frame to frame. If, however, you use the second method, and I think it is a little easier and quicker in the long run, the centre pieces should all be the same length from the water line but as long as they are all the same the actual length does not matter.

Mark the load water line and sheer line on the frame in pencil and the job is done. Repeat the process for the remaining frames. Like most jobs it sounds far more complicated than it is.

There are two simple ways of making the strong back; I will describe them both. The first method assumes that your timber is rather twisted and conditions generally are a bit rough. For the second method you have to be able to make the centre timber of your strong back fairly straight and flat. Using the first method the strong back is quickly made from 8″ × 2″ with some 4″ and 6″ nails and a heavy hammer. Fig. 3 shows the idea.

As far as possible the outside pieces of timber should be placed so that the frames will rest on them. The timber we used was pretty badly warped, and the concrete it was laid on was none too even, so we had to use packing to get the strong back reasonably square and firm. Provided that you can jump up and down on the strong back without it moving and that the centre piece of timber is within an inch or two of where it should be everything is O.K. It is a great help as well if it can be made more or less level.

Measure and mark with a pencil the frame positions on the centre timber of the strong back. Firmly nail or screw pieces of 2″ × 1″ down the side of the centre member of the strong back at these marks. The centre timber of each frame is going to be screwed to these so make sure that they are at right angles to the centre line. If the strong back has been levelled you can use a spirit level for this, otherwise a try square

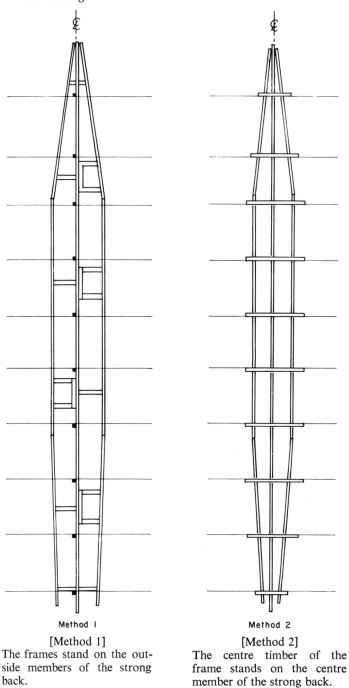

Method 1   Method 2

[Method 1]   [Method 2]
The frames stand on the out-   The centre timber of the
side members of the strong   frame stands on the centre
back.   member of the strong back.

Fig. 3.   The two types of strong back. Note how the frames are behind the position line in the front half of the hull and in front of them in the rear half.

and eye, but a spirit level is much easier and surer. They need to be on the correct side of the line, otherwise you may find that, because your frames are cut square rather than to follow the curve of the hull, your hull is a bit wider than it should be (Fig. 4). A piece of string stretched from end to end is used to give a centre line.

The quickest way to set up the frames is to have three people and two G-cramps. One or two people with three G-cramps have no problem, it just takes longer, because there is so much walking and cramping to be done. The order in which the frames are set up is not important but the most practical way is to erect one near either end of the mould then fill in the middle.

Let us assume that you are going to set up frame 2 first, followed by frame 9.

Place pieces of one-inch-thick timber on the outer members of the strong back where the ends of frame 2 are going to rest. This is to allow for any irregularities in the strong back timber as you work back. If this allowance is not made it is quite possible that frame 2 will be at a particularly low part of the strong back and you will then have to saw lumps off all the other frames to make them line up.

Stand the frame up and cramp it to the correct side of the 2″ × 1″ on the centre member of the strong back. Pull out the packing from under the outsides of the frame and cramp short lengths of 2″ × 1″ to extend the frame to meet the strong back. Using a spirit level and try square adjust the cramps until the frame is upright and perpendicular to the general lie of the strong back, and the centre piece of 2″ × 1″ is just touching the centre string.

Nail a piece of timber from some way up the centre 2″ × 1″ to the strong back to hold the frame upright while you drill and screw it securely to the strong back. Put a couple of No. 10 screws through the centre 2″ × 1″, two more in each of the extension pieces and two more diagonally through the extension pieces into the strong back. An electric drill with a counter-bore bit and pump screwdriver, all of which will be needed later anyway, speed up this part of the operation.

Take frame 9 and cramp short 2″ × 1″ extensions to the sides of the frame. Then cramp the centre member of the frame to the appropriate block on the strong back.

If you step back a few yards you will be able to sight through frame 9 to frame 2; it is simply a matter of adjusting the cramps on frame 9 until the sighting pieces on the two frames line up exactly.

Obviously both frames should be just touching the centre-line string and at right angles to it across the strong back. We used a try square to get our frames at right angles to the centre-line string, not terribly accurate by engineering standards but more than adequate for practical boat-building purposes.

Make sure that frame 9 is also perpendicular to the strong back. This is done most easily with a spirit level, if you have been able to make the strong back more or less level, otherwise you will have to use a try square.

Screw the frame into place and remove the cramps.

The remaining frames are erected in the same way. We found when sighting along

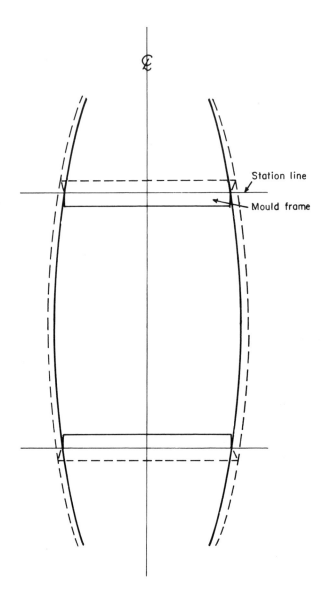

Station line

Mould frame

Fig. 4. Exaggerated diagram to show how the mould frames must be on the correct side of the station line marked on the strong back. The dotted lines show how the hull could be distorted. This distortion would obviously not be very significant over thirty or forty feet, but it is better to try and get things right from the beginning.

9. This is how Derek Kelsall made the mould for the main hull of one of his trimarans, seen from the inside.

the frames that if we were at all uncertain about them being lined up correctly they were not, but when all the sighting and centre lines were as they should be there was no doubt at all.

We also found it much easier to pack up the outsides of the frames with scraps of wood and make one large final adjustment with the cramp just before screwing up, rather than to try to adjust the cramp each time.

With two of us and three cramps our frames took nearly an hour each to set up. This was mainly because so much time was spent walking backwards and forwards between sighting and making adjustments. A third person to sight and call out directions while the other two make the necessary adjustments cuts this time dramatically to something under a quarter of an hour for each frame.

The second method for erecting the frame calls for the centre member of the strong back to be quite flat. What happens to the timber between the frame position is not important of course, just as long as there are four or five inches of fair timber at each frame position and all the frame positions are true to each other. This can be achieved either by packing up or planning down the centre timber. Use a good tight string, or simply sight along, to make sure they are true.

The outer members of the strong back should be placed so that they are completely inside the frame timbers. Measure and mark the exact frame positions on the strong back and nail 2″ × 1″ across the strong back on the correct side of these lines. The frames will be screwed to these so they need to extend beyond the outside of the strong back far enough for this to be done.

The frames are now erected as they were in the first method except that the centre timber of the frame stands on the centre member of the strong back rather than down the side of it and the outsides of the frames are screwed to the pieces of 2″ × 1″ nailed across the strong back. You may still find it necessary to pack up or pare down the centre line 2″ × 1″ to make the frames line up.

These are just two methods of doing the job; you may know of others or you might prefer to work a system made up from parts of both described methods.

The important points are that the frames should be reasonably lined up and square, and that the finished mould should be strong enough to support the weight of the foam and resinglass you are going to put on it. From the strength point of view, either the centre timber or the outsides of the frames should rest directly on top of the strong back.

Once all the frames are in position the stem piece can be made from 6″ × 1″. The number of pieces necessary to make the stem will depend entirely on the shape of the stem.

If the stem has a lot of shape it might even pay to draw it out full size on a piece of hardboard and make it up in the same way as the frames. Otherwise one or two measurements can be taken from the lines drawing and the stem drawn directly on to some 6″ × 1″ tacked between the first frame and the stem head. Once you are satisfied that you have the right shape, screw the stem piece between the frame and the strong back.

On craft with very fine entries and narrow hulls, like catamarans and trimarans, it might be necessary to use a piece of 6″ × 1″ between the first two frames as well, to give the keel line. This might also be necessary on a mono-hull with lots of shape at the bow and stern. Once the frames are in place it becomes obvious where you need extra 6″ × 1″ and where you can do without it.

The 1″ × 1″ stringers go on next. Put two stringers along the keel close together, but far enough apart to get a pencil through, then you can go along just before you take the hull off the mould and mark a centre line inside the hull. It is also a good idea to put stringers along the sheer line and water line at this stage. Do not try to make the latter follow round at the stern if it does not want to. We made sure the keel and sheer were fair before proceeding with the bulk of the battening just so that the other stringers would not interfere with our view of the important lines.

It is important to check that you can actually get inside the mould under the sheer-

10. Here is the same mould as Plate 9 seen from the outside. The sort of strong back they use at Sandwich Marina can be seen quite clearly.

line stringer. A piece can be cut out of the strong back if you have miscalculated somewhere, but if the frames have been extended this should not be necessary.

The gap between the stringers is not at all important except that it should be narrower on tight curves than large flat areas. If you tend to run your stringers from one end of the mould to the other you will in fact find that they are almost touching at stem and stern where there is most curvature and quite open amidships where there is usually less curvature.

A gap of about three inches seems right for curves of about twelve-inch radius, opening to a gap of six inches on flat areas.

To make sure the stringers do not pull the hull out of shape it is a good idea to work on each side of the hull more or less at the same time, never having more than three stringers more on one side of the mould than on the other.

The stringers can be screwed at either end and then nailed to the frames in the middle, which is quick, and the easiest way if you are planning to break your mould out from inside the hull, rather than to lift the hull off the mould. Or the stringers can be screwed to each frame—a much surer method if you are planning to use the mould more than once and it makes it much easier to put packing under the stringers when you come to fair up the mould. If you have any doubts about the fairness of your frames, because of either poor drawings or the quality of your own woodworking, it will almost certainly pay you to use screws.

The lines drawings we had to work from were really good, but the cutting of the frames was nothing spectacular I am afraid, so it took three of us about ten hours to fair up our mould.

A flexible batten held round the stringers and an eye-sighting along soon show up any that need attention. The frame can be chiselled away if a stringer is proud, and for stringers that are low, pieces of thin plywood between the stringer and frame do the trick. If the mould is to be used more than once the packing needs to be fixed so that it can not shift. Glue can be used or the packing can be drilled and the screw holding the

11.   Starting to put the stringers on the mould. Notice that the stringers have been put on first on one side of the mould and then on the other to avoid distorting the mould. Because of the tight curves on a dinghy like this we had to use $\frac{3}{4}''$-square timber for the stringers.

40

12. Drilling the stringers ready to screw on the foam. These stringers are a bit too far apart, as we found out when we put the foam on.

You can see where we had to chisel the first frame quite drastically to get the mould fair, and if you look closely at the second frame you will see that most of the stringers have been packed up some distance from the frame. All this was necessary because I refused to believe my drawings.

stringer put through the packing as well. We used this latter method and found it worked very well. Derek Kelsall uses glue and that also works very well. You pays your money. . . .

The stringers now have to be drilled for the screws that will hold the foam in place, No. 10 screws are the size used. The holes want to be big enough so that you can push a screw through without any effort yet small enough so the screw does not fall out when you let go, something like $\frac{7}{32}''$ should be ideal.

Drill holes about every three inches where the stringers are close together and less frequently in the flatter areas, say every twelve inches in completely flat areas like the sides of a catamaran hull.

That completes the mould but before you start putting on the foam it is a good idea to mark the positions of any bulkheads you might have, on both the inside and outside of the stringers.

On these marks make bulkhead templates from cardboard. These will have to be reduced to allow for the inner skin of resinglass, and you will find life much easier when you come to fit the bulkheads if they are on the small side. Little wedges can be used to hold the bulkheads in place in the hull. Doing things this way also means that you can have your bulkheads ready before you lift your hull off the mould, which is a good thing.

SPECIAL MOULDS FOR CATAMARANS

If you are making a catamaran with accommodation on the bridge deck between the hulls you will need to make a mould for the fillet that joins the bridge deck to the hulls (Fig. 5). You will also need to cut formers to the curve of the front of the bridge deck.

13. This photograph of our first hull being lifted off the mould shows how the hull is shaped where the bridge deck joins. This piece is made on a separate mould, and for want of a better title we christened it the 'fillet moulding'.

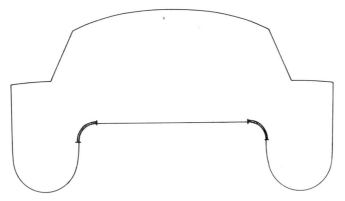

Fig. 5. Typical section of a catamaran showing the quadrant fillets between the hulls and the bridge deck which have to be moulded before the main hull mould is covered with foam.

The fillet mould is half round in section and as long as the joint between the bridge deck and hull at its longest plus a couple of feet to allow for cutting. This is the easiest way but as this length has to be cut up eventually it is quite possible to make a much shorter mould, say six or eight feet long and work on this, in a garage perhaps before the weather gets warm enough to work outside.

Resinglass shrinks as it cures and unless you use short lengths of $1'' \times 1''$ with pieces of plywood nailed on the ends, or something similar, across the open side of the half round when you take it off the mould, it will in fact flatten out considerably within a week or two (Fig. 6).

Foam and resinglass are laid on this mould in the same way as the hull.

When the resin has cured the moulding can be sawn longitudinally down its middle to make two quadrant fillets, one for each hull. Do not resinglass the inside of this moulding—that will be done at the same time as the outside of the hull. This fillet has to be made and positioned before any foam is put on the hull mould.

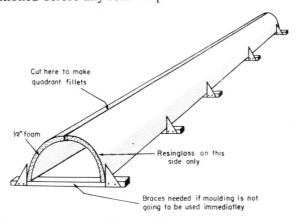

Cut here to make
quadrant fillets

½" foam

Resinglass on this
side only

Braces needed if moulding is not
going to be used immediatley

Fig. 6. Section of fillet after taking it off the mould.

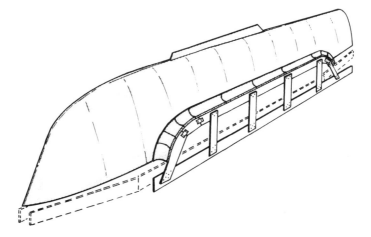

Fig. 7. Side view of a catamaran mould showing fillet in place on a support made from 6″ × 1″ or similar.

Remembering that it will all have to be transferred to the other side of the mould, rig up some sort of support for the fillet at the correct height and distance from the hull mould (Fig. 7). Some 6″ × 1″ timber on edge with two or three supports to the ground is strong enough; it can be curved to follow the line of the hull and held in place with struts to the frames of the main mould.

Draw out the curve of the front end of the bridge deck full size and cut a couple of formers from 6″ × 1″ to fit. Having already made your hull mould this will be child's play. These formers can be screwed to the fillet support and braced to the main mould to support the front end of the fillet and give it its curve.

We tried drawing the curve on the main mould and working to that, but is was not very successful and I would recommend cutting formers (which you will need eventually to make the bridge deck anyway) and using these (Fig. 8).

Cover the fillet support with polythene, or resin will run back under the fillet and stick fillet and support firmly together. Please don't ask me how I know!

Now start putting the fillet in place. You will probably find that you have to saw the flat centre section into three or four pieces to get it to fit the curve of the hull. Hold the pieces in place by screwing through from inside the mould and if necessary use a few nails through the edge of the fillet into the support; leave the heads of any nails used clear so that you can pull them out later.

Where the bridge deck curves at the bow end the easiest thing is to cut the fillet into pieces about twelve to eighteen inches long. Position these on the formers, again screwing from inside the main mould. This will leave a series of triangular gaps. Spare fillet moulding can now be cut to fill these gaps.

If, like us, you have a curved back to your cockpit, proceed exactly as you did at the front end; only because the curve is so tight, a twelve-inch radius in our case, the pieces must be much narrower—four inches seemed about right for us. The joints need fairing up with resin putty and sand paper but this is readily done and offers no problems.

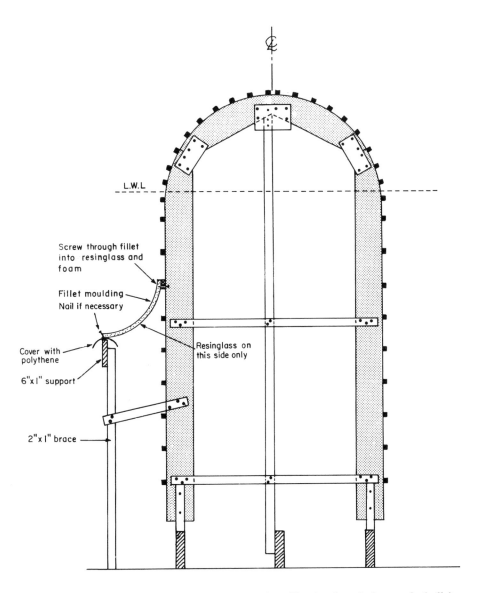

Fig. 8. Typical section of a catamaran mould showing fillet in place before main hull is covered with foam.

Putting on the Foam

The foam is bent over the mould and held in place with No. 10 wood screws from inside the mould. In some places you may find it easier to tie the foam to the mould stringers with fishing line or nail through the foam into the mould, but screws do the bulk of the work.

Gaps between the sheets of foam are then filled with resin putty and the whole thing generally tidied up.

In the chapter on materials you will find that I have discussed at some length the various types of foam available and their different merits. But in this chapter I shall be dealing with Airex, rigid P.V.C. foam, which is the material we used throughout and which is the foam Derek Kelsall uses and recommends.

The foam we used was 12 mm. thick. The density was 5·29 pounds per cubic foot approximately and it comes in sheets between seven and eight feet long and three and four feet wide. The thickness and density vary a bit from sheet to sheet but this does not seem to make any difference.

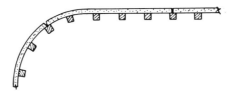

Fig. 9.   Sheets of foam joined where there is considerable curvature leave an open seam. Much better to join in a relatively flat area.

Start putting the foam on at the centre of the mould and work towards the ends. Try to avoid having joints in the foam where the hull has considerable curvature (Fig. 9), and have the top and bottom of the sheets of foam supported by mould stringers (Fig. 10). Although it is not vital it does not hurt to stagger the joints between the sheets. For speed in fairing up, the sheets should be as large as possible, but the size is ultimately dictated by the degree of curvature of the hull. We found we could use 4′ ×8′ sheets for the middle half of our hulls without any trouble, but where the curves started to tighten up at the ends we had to cut the sheets down to two feet in width.

At different times were tried one, two and three people in the team putting on the foam. With one person it was a slow business with pieces of wood and cramps, though if you are thinking of working solo it should be possible to leave a slightly wider gap between the stringers so that you can get your arm through; using two foot wide strips of foam, sew the foam to the stringers from the outside using nylon fishing line. With three people in the team there was a decided waste of man power. Two people, one inside using the screwdriver, one outside pressing on the foam, were ideal.

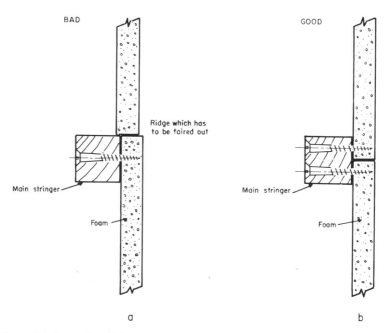

Fig. 10.   If possible foam should be cut so that it rests against a stringer, as in diagram b. Both pieces of foam are supported by mould stringer.

Lay your first piece of foam on the mould to get some idea of where it comes to. Standing inside the mould, push No. 10 steel countersunk head wood screws through the holes drilled in the mould stringers over the area of the first piece of foam. The screws should be as long as possible, but not so long that they come through the outside of the foam. The actual length is dictated by the thickness of the stringers and foam. To get some idea of just how many screws are needed to hold the foam down I suggest initially you put screws in every other hole, rather than in every hole.

Now, assuming that there are two of you (as the stuff is very light a woman or boy can help if you cannot get another man), body number one lays the foam on the mould and applies pressure, trying not to dent the foam, while body number two pushes the screws home from inside the mould with a big pump screwdriver. Start with the keel, and, working along each stringer from end to end as you go, move down the mould on one side. Then do the other side.

The foam is fairly soft so the screws go in easily, but it is also very easy to over-tighten the screws so that they tear out of the foam. If a screw does tear out all you have to do is move it to the next hole and try again. After a few screws we found we could judge fairly accurately the amount of pressure needed to pull the foam to the stringers without tearing the screws out.

Once you have the first piece of foam on examine it closely from inside the mould. If it is lying snugly against the stringers everywhere all is well. The chances are, however, especially if you have not put screws in every hole, that in some areas the foam will be lifting away from the stringers slightly. A few more screws in these areas should do the trick.

If your hull is very small, or making floats for a trimaran, it is possible an eight-foot length of foam will go from one gunwale to the other, in which case it is a simple matter to trim the foam with a sharp knife so that it is flush with the gunwale stringer. Normally you will find that your first pieces of foam are some feet short of the gunwale. In this case use a straight edge and trim the foam to the most convenient batten; expose at least a quarter of an inch of batten for the lower piece of foam to rest on, otherwise it will tend to curl into the mould and you will have problems trying to push it out again (Fig. 10).

Now that you have some idea of how frequently the foam needs screwing to hold it to the curves of your particular boat, you can work through the hull pushing screws into the stringers.

We used 24 gross on our hull, but I think we tended to be a bit extravagant. To work out how many screws to buy all I did was look at the largest section on the lines drawing and work out roughly how many stringers there would be at that part of the mould. I then assumed that all these stringers would run the full length of the mould and that on average every stringer would have a screw in it every four inches. The resulting number seemed so astronomical that I had to work the sum out three or four different ways before I was convinced. Once convinced I added on another couple of gross for luck and they were not wasted.

We also had three or four gross of longer screws to use where the stringers were doubled at the joints.

Fortunately all these screws only have to be screwed into soft foam so, although the number is considerable, the work is in fact light.

If you are making a normal sort of mono-hull or the centre hull of a trimaran, it does not really matter whether you put foam all down the back of the mould and then fill in along the gunwale or fill in along the gunwale as you go. On a largish catamaran, however, which has big flat areas on the outboard sides of its hulls, it is advisable to put foam on the curved areas of the mould and then pre-resinglass the flat panels before putting them on the mould, but more about that later. For this reason I shall assume you are going to work along the hull rather than round it.

Boats being the shape they are you will probably find that, if you put another piece of foam on the mould so that it butts up to the first piece at the keel, as you pull the second piece down to the mould it will start to overlap the first piece. This overlap has to be cut off so that the two pieces butt together, although the quality of the fit is of no real importance. If you have a lot of gaps it just means you will have to spend a little more time with the resin putty and slithers of foam.

We came to the conclusion that it was quicker to cut with a small gap, i.e. $\frac{1}{16}''$ or $\frac{1}{8}''$, and fill later than it was to try to fit accurately in the first place.

The method for fitting we adopted, after various experiments involving marking through from within the mould, was simply to arrange the piece of foam so that the overlaps looked about even on both sides of the hull. The screws were then driven home along the two keel stringers, and in any other stringers available, before the foam started to overlap the preceding piece. With the person inside the mould helping to hold the bottom of the foam in place, the man outside the mould could then run a

14. The first piece of foam has been screwed into place while the second piece has been screwed on at the keel and is ready for cutting. Because the curves on the dinghy were so tight we had to use narrow pieces of foam; on a larger boat larger pieces of foam can be used, which is much quicker.

knife down cutting off the overlap. With a little practice we found we could use the under piece of foam as a guide without actually cutting into it and so get pretty good joints that needed the minimum of filling.

Once this side had been screwed down, the operation was repeated on the other side of the hull. Working in this way it is quick and easy to get even the largest mould covered with foam.

Eventually, as you work towards the bow, you will come to a point where the hull has a sharp line at the keel. It is quite straight-forward to cut the foam and join it at this line so that it makes a reasonable shape.

Also at the bow, depending on how sharp it is, you will eventually find that you cannot screw into the foam from within the mould. Do not make the mistake of putting screws into the first side of foam which you will not be able to get out when the other side of the bow is in place. No, that was one clanger we did not drop.

The trick here is either to screw the foam down from the outside or to sew it together with nylon fishing line. Derek Kelsall tends to use nylon. As we had neither line nor large needles, but we did have lots of screws, we used screws. I think this was probably a mistake, and a couple of long needles with some twelve or fifteen pounds' breaking-strain fishing line would have been a good investment.

The main snag with using nylon line is that you cannot sand down the foam without cutting the line. If you are going to break the mould out of the hull 1″ round wire nails can be hammered through the foam into the stringers where necessary. These nails can be pulled through the foam when the mould is broken out. They leave holes in the foam but within reason these are nothing to worry about.

If you use screws you will find that you have to screw them in until they bury themselves right into the foam. Put a little spot of barrier cream or vaseline on to each screw head after it has been screwed home. Otherwise the slots get filled with resin, which all has to be laboriously chipped out before you can remove the screws.

Remove the screws and fill all the holes once the first layer of resinglass has gone off. Or, if you have a long line of screws on either side of the bow, as we had, it is a good idea to put a six-inch wide strip of mat over the joint and then remove the screws. This saves time later when you are trying to get your second layer of resinglass on the first within the twenty-four hours' time limit.

There is nothing wrong or bad in using screws from the outside, it is simply that they involve a lot of work in drilling out and hole filling which can be avoided if you stitch pieces of foam together and to the mould.

Once the foam is on the mould it has to be faired up. This involves going round inside and outside the mould to see where the foam is not sitting snugly on the mould stringers.

In areas where the foam is lifting a little it might be necessary to put in a few extra screws, or it might simply be a question of tightening the existing ones slightly.

We found that the edges of our sheets of foam tended to curl away from the mould

15.   How she looked from the inside with the foam in place.

and we had to put a series of screws into each sheet, about half an inch in from the edge. To drill the batten without going through the foam it is simply a matter of wrapping some masking tape round the drill bit the appropriate distance from its point. But here again I think it would be much quicker to stitch the edges of the two sheets of foam to the mould battens, provided you arm yourself with the necessary materials before you start.

All joints in the foam need filling with resin putty. Resin putty can be bought ready made. But it is cheaper, especially as you are buying resin at bulk prices, to buy a suitable filler powder from your resin supplier and use this in your normal lay-up resin.

We found it most convenient to mix up a bucketful of putty at a time. Catalyst was not added to this of course. Then, as needed, we catalysed a small quantity of the putty in a plastic container. We only catalysed a small amount at a time and never found any need to measure the catalyst; we simply added a few drops and hoped. Because the quantity of resin in the putty is so small there is no chance of the mix being under-catalysed, nor is there much chance of it going hard before you have had a chance to use it.

We used a variety of instruments for putting on the resin putty, ranging from glazier's putty knives, to steel rulers and ordinary dinner knives. We even tried odd scraps of perspex. They all worked, but a two-inch stripping knife gave the best results, though the glazier's putty knife was nearly as good.

Whatever tools you decide to use, clean them with acetone before the putty goes hard, otherwise you will have to grind it off or break it off with a hammer. Hammering breaks dinner knives and bends glazier's knives, so use acetone.

Even the best fitting joints should have a quick wipe with the putty knife, otherwise resin seeps through and sticks the foam firmly to the mould. Yes, I am talking from experience. A good stiff mix of resin putty can be used on gaps of up to about an eighth of an inch wide, but over this size we found it easier, and quicker, to stuff the gap with thin offcuts of foam first.

Where foam of slightly differing thicknesses meet, the difference must be faired out, either by building up with resin putty or by rubbing down the thicker pieces. Perhaps I should add that with Airex we found any difference to be very slight and, for all practical purposes, most of the sheets we had were all the same thickness.

Glass cloth will not fit over an angle without leaving an air bubble. So all sharp corners, e.g. at the transom, bow, or knuckle line, have to be softened. Three-eighths of an inch seems to be about the minimum safe radius, 18 oz. undirectional woven roving will follow (Fig. 11). To be absolutely certain we rubbed all our angles down to a radius of about half an inch.

Edge tools, like planes and chisels, work quite well on Airex foam but they have to be very sharp, which is rather awkward because the foam seems to blunt a plane as quickly as any hard wood. Perhaps it is just a question of experimenting with sharpening angles; anyway there are alternatives.

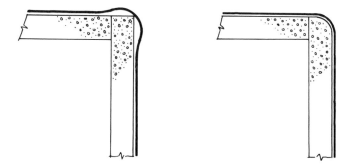

Fig. 11.   If you try and put resinglass round a sharp corner it forms a weak bubble along the angle. Three-eighths of an inch is about the minimum radius that 18 oz. undirectional roving will follow without trouble.

16. All the foam is on and all the seams have been filled. You can see that we used nails to hold the transom in place and that the angle where the side and transom meet has been well rounded.

Coarse aluminium oxide sandpaper works quite well. We used 16-grit discs in ordinary electric hand drills to remove the bulk of the excess foam, finishing by hand with 60-grit paper. We found that finer grit discs, especially if used at high speed, tended to gouge lumps out of the foam unless handled extremely carefully. The coarse paper shows this tendency as well but not to the same extent as the fine.

Surform tools are all right for working on foam, but they are rather expensive and blunt almost as quickly as a plane iron.

Within reason the more time you spend making sure the hull is fair at this stage the more time you will save in subsequent operations. But above all make sure that there are no sharp edges for the resinglass to go over or little nobs in the resin putty you have used to fill the joints in the foam.

We spent about fifty hours putting the foam on our hull and a further fifty hours doing the tidying up. This includes a certain amount of time for finding out how to do things.

FOAM: SPECIAL CONSIDERATIONS

Boats with large flat areas along the top sides, and here I am thinking particularly of catamarans, need something to stiffen them a bit, otherwise they flop about all over the place when the hull is taken off the mould.

We did two things. First we had a piece of $2'' \times \frac{1}{2}''$ mahogany along the gunwale instead of foam. Second, and far more important, we put one layer of 18 oz. resinglass on the *inside* of the foam in these areas.

To do this first cover the mould with foam, using just enough screws in the flat areas to support the foam. Once all the foam has been fitted the flat pieces are numbered and removed and the *inside* resinglassed with one layer of 18 oz. undirectional woven

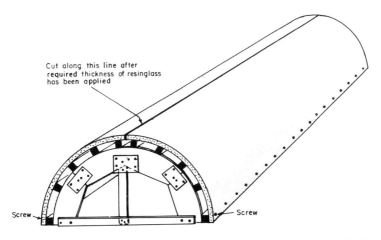

Fig. 12. Catamaran hull/bridge deck fillet mould. It is only necessary to hold foam to mould with screws in bottom stringers.

roving. When this has hardened it is scuffed-up with a 24-grit aluminium-oxide disc. It is much easier to do the grinding at this stage rather than later when the hull has been made and turned over. These pre-resinglassed panels are then replaced on the mould. Instead of using a screwdriver for the screws it is easier to hit them in with a hammer, just giving a slight turn with the screwdriver at the end to make sure.

If you are making a catamaran with a fillet between the hull and bridge deck as described earlier you will need to make this fillet before you put foam on the hull mould. The fillet mould will only have a simple curve and we found it unnecessary to put hundreds of screws in it.

We simply screwed the foam to the bottom stringer of the mould on each side from the outside (Fig. 12). Before we put any resinglass on the foam we put a little dab of barrier cream on each screwhead to stop the slots getting gummed up with resin.

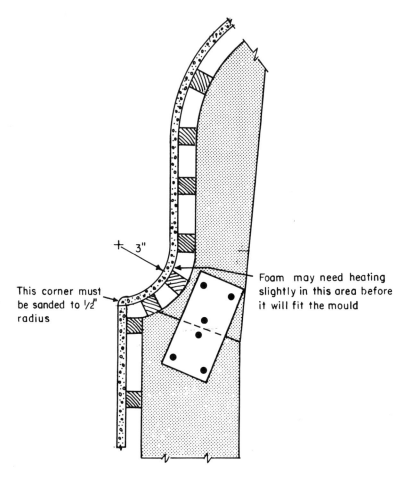

This corner must be sanded to ½" radius

Foam may need heating slightly in this area before it will fit the mould

Fig. 13. Section through a mould with a knuckle in the hull.

56

To avoid the chore of drilling the resinglass to get the screws out we stopped it a couple of inches short of the screw holes.

It is possible that the design you are making has curves which are tighter than it is possible to bend P.V.C. foam to in the normal way. The most likely place for this is a knuckle line with a three- or four-inch radius band (Fig. 13).

A little heat in the appropriate place is all that is needed. P.V.C. foam placed in hot water, in front of a fire or with hot air blowing on to it, quickly softens and can easily be bent to the tightest of curves. You might even find that your wife's hair dryer is hot enough; mine has not got one so I have not been able to do any experiments.

Resinglass

Now we come to the rather controversial subject of resinglass, and the conditions necessary to use the stuff successfully.

Lloyd's, in their booklet on glass-reinforced plastic boat building, suggest that resin should be used only in the temperature range of 16°C. to 21°C. (60°F. to 70°F.)—though the temperature can drop after laying up, i.e. during the night, to 10°C. (50°F.); and the relative humidity should not exceed 65 to 70 per cent.

There are, however, users of resinglass, Hugo du Plessis being one, who point out that this is only the ideal temperature range and that for all practical purposes resinglass is so strong that if the lay up is conscientiously done all will be well provided the temperature is something above freezing point. It is, however, necessary that the glass is absolutely dry before use and that new resin work is protected from moisture. The plan we adopted was to work during the time of year when the temperature was likely to be within the Lloyd's range but not to worry if it was not, and to provide a polythene shelter to keep rain and dew off. We were unable to carry out sophisticated strength tests on our sandwich but crude testing of offcuts showed that failure, when it did eventually occur, was within the structure of the foam and not in the resinglass skin or in the bond between the resinglass and foam. The finished sandwich was strong by any standards.

It is worth bearing in mind that factors other than the conditions under which it is done determine the strength of a resinglass lay-up; here the amateur should score because he is not bound by the same time-cost considerations as the professional boat moulders and he is much more strongly motivated towards doing a first-class job than any lay-up hand working for a weekly wage.

The ratio of resin to glass and the degree of wetting out of the glass both have a large bearing on the strength of the lay-up. Provided the glass is thoroughly wetted out, i.e. the resin has penetrated to the very core of the glass strands, the *less* resin that is used the stronger the lay-up. Professional moulders generally aim for a ratio of $2\frac{1}{2}$ to 3 lb. of resin to 1 lb. of chopped strand mat, or $1\frac{1}{2}$ to 2 lb. of resin (and this is one reason why it is stronger) to 1 lb. of woven roving.

Because of its higher strength, woven roving of one sort or another is used more extensively in foam-sandwich construction than in normal moulding. Our boat is no exception to this and the bulk of our glass was 18 oz. undirectional woven roving. We found that we needed 2 lb. of resin for each pound of woven roving when we started, but after a little practice we were able to reduce this by 4 oz. to 1 lb. 12 oz. It simply meant we had to brush a little harder.

We found with the chopped strand mat that we could reduce the resin to $2\frac{1}{4}$ lb. for each pound of glass, but to get down to this ratio we had to do some hard rolling. As we used only a small quantity of chopped strand mat (about 180 lb.), and this for reinforcing stressed areas, we opted for the lower resin content with the corresponding gain in strength and did the extra rolling required, which in these quantities really is not all that much.

A point worth remembering here is that a resin-starved, poorly wetted out lay-up is weaker than a lay-up which is moderately resin rich. So we never hesitated to put extra resin on an area of glass that was not wetting out properly, even though it had already had its quota of resin by weight. Mostly we found that if the quantity of resin was calculated roughly beforehand, and a bit added on to allow for drips, etc., extra resin was not necessary. Trying to work at speed on an almost vertical surface can easily give a resin wastage of 5 or 10 per cent, but most surfaces are not vertical and wastage is quite low—1 or 2 per cent.

I am convinced that just about anyone, almost anywhere in the world, can use resin and glass fibre successfully without air-conditioned premises, provided they use a bit of common sense. In England this means rigging up some sort of shelter to keep the rain and dew off the resin and only working during the warmer months of the year, though I found it possible to work during the autumn, before the first frost, by getting all my resin work done by about 1400 hrs. waiting for it to gell, then covering it with two or three layers of dry newspaper and a polythene sheet. The newspaper keeps the resin warm and absorbs any moisture there might be about.

If you live in a cold part of the world, but where electricity is cheap, you might consider using electric blankets for this job.

If you want to build in the tropics you will need a shelter to keep the sun off the moulding and you may have to think about doing resin work after dark—in direct sunlight resin gells very quickly indeed, so quickly in fact that there is not enough time to wet out the glass completely, and the resin can get so hot it boils, leaving big bubbles in the lay-up.

But wherever you build, you will almost certainly have to get used to the idea of varying the amount of catalyst you use for every pound of resin, to allow for temperature variations. The actual amount of catalyst will vary with different resin from different manufacturers, but keep a thermometer handy and you will quickly get to know how much catalyst is needed to give a reasonable working life.

We used a gelling time of about thirty minutes, but when working alone I found it paid to extend the time to nearer forty-five minutes. Resin that has not gone off within one-and-a-half to two hours is under-catalysed for the existing temperature and something should be done to warm it up a bit. We never had to do this in fact, but I imagine a domestic electric fan heater would do the trick.

60

Long gelling times should be avoided, especially with the first layer of resinglass in contact with the foam. The longer the resinglass is soft, the greater the chance there is of it absorbing moisture from the atmosphere, but even more important is the softening effect that ungelled resin has on P.V.C. foam. This softening is one of those things you should know about, but in practical terms we did not find it anything to worry about. Derek Kelsall comments on this. 'You will find from time to time that the foam has softened due to the styrene in the resin and the softening may remain for a period of a few days, but in each and every case that I have come across this has disappeared after about one week. Samples that I have made up especially that have been extremely soft have all become rigid finally.' Resin that takes a long time to go off also loses some strength, but again this is of more academic than practical interest.

We needed between 2 and 5 cc. of catalyst for every pound of resin but your resin supplier will give you the safe limits for his particular brand. It is advisable to stay more or less within these limits otherwise the strength could be affected, though here again your own supplier should be able to advise on this, even if he insists that the advice be considered 'off the record' as it were. It should be safe to use up to four or five times the amount of catalyst you need at a temperature of 65°F.

The technique for putting on the resinglass is straightforward and it requires no previous experience, though we found we did the job quicker and with less effort after some practice.

A team of three is just about ideal for doing the resinglass work. We found, however, that one or two people could do it without trouble, it just took longer.

Briefly the order of working is: measure and cut the glass; weigh the resin; catalyse the resin; brush resin on to the foam; unroll the glass on to the wet resin; brush on more resin; give finishing touches where necessary.

After two or three pieces of glass you should find the whole operation as simple and as quick as it sounds. The following detailed notes and descriptions are given to help you with those first few pieces of glass and possibly as you gain experience and confidence you will modify the methods I suggest to suit your particular conditions.

Unless your hull is so small that you can stand on the ground and reach the keel, you will need some sort of scaffolding to stand on. Initially we tried using step-ladders but, while possible, they wasted a great deal of time. Therefore when we came to do our second hull, we made four trestles from some old $3'' \times \frac{3}{4}''$ timber. The trestles were about four feet high and with 12 ft.-long scaffold boards placed on these we could reach the keel quite comfortably and more or less walk the full length of the hull. Our boards were about nine inches wide which was adequate; we had one or two close shaves, but nobody actually fell off.

When everything is set up, measure out and cut your first length of glass. On our boat we have an extra layer of 18 oz. undirectional woven roving running from stem to stern along the keel and this was the first piece we put on. However, prior to this we had had some practice using resin when we made our bridge deck fillet and pre-glassed

61

our topside panels.

If you can find a nice long table on which to cut your glass so much the better but we managed quite well working at ground level. To support our roll of glass we pushed a piece of wood, longer than the roll, through the middle and rested the protruding ends on a couple of blocks of wood. Rolls of glass are heavy so the wood has to be strong, metal pipe would be better, but we could not find a piece long enough and at the time it did not seem worth while to go and buy a piece.

We had an old piece of plywood 5′ × 2′ for cutting on and nailed to the top of this was a piece of batten, marked off in feet, for measuring the glass as it was unrolled (Fig. 14). On either side of the piece of ply we put cardboard, from the glass cartons, on the ground to keep the glass clean. The glass can be marked with an ordinary pencil as it is measured off and we found it a good idea to have a piece of masking tape somewhere close by on which to keep a tally—otherwise, with fourteen-yard lengths of cloth, we could easily have forgotten how many yards we had counted off and would have had to remeasure.

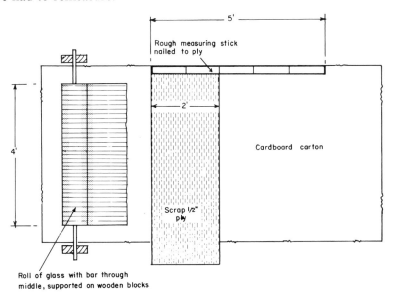

Fig. 14. Our glass-cutting 'table'.

As the glass is measured it should be rolled up. While working on the outside of the hull we found it best if the end of the glass was taped and rolled on to one of the cardboard cores on which the glass is delivered. When working inside the hull, however, this is not really possible and the glass just has to be rolled on itself.

A sharp Stanley knife is good for cutting the glass but the blades blunt fairly quickly. Rather than use a new blade every time this happened we found it just as quick and much cheaper to sharpen the existing blade on a fine oilstone.

We were using Marglass 280 which is an 18 oz. undirectional woven roving. This glass cloth has some threads of terylene, or something similar, along its edge. Without this the glass cloth frays badly along the edge, it just falls apart in fact. So, before cutting the glass, put a strip of one-inch wide masking tape across the cloth with an inch or so sticking over at each side to stop the edges fraying. You can get away with using two short pieces of tape, one on each edge of the cloth, but this is rather fiddly. Masking tape is not very expensive and a strip right across the cloth gives a good guide for cutting. Cut down the middle of the masking tape so that all ends are protected by half an inch of tape.

If you cut along the length of the cloth for any reason you will find the cut edge frays very badly unless you have put a length of masking tape on first, which you then cut down the middle.

Leave any masking tape on until the cloth is fully wetted out with resin, then it will more or less fall off without pulling too much of the glass with it. This is especially important where the tape runs along the length of the cloth.

Next weigh out the total quantity of resin you will need for the piece of glass. The glass we used was four feet wide which, at 18 oz. to the square yard, works out very conveniently to half a pound for each foot run.

Using a small spring balance we weighed our resin direct from the 500 lb. drum into plastic buckets in 9 lb. lots. Initially we worked with 2 lb. of resin to 1 lb. of glass and this amount of resin was always necessary when putting the first layer of resinglass on to the foam, With practice we managed to reduce the resin content by about 4 oz. when putting resinglass on resinglass.

In the final stages of building we tried a thin marine resin and found that we could use this at a ratio of a pound of resin to a pound of glass. This thin resin penetrated the glass much more easily than the thicker one we had been using and required less effort on our part to achieve full wetting out. Each bucket of resin is catalysed as it is needed, and a plastic dispenser for the catalyst is a must when working with large quantities of resin like this.

We kept the catalyst by the resin drum and never came even close to forgetting to put it in, though going on the books I have read it seems as though amateurs are expected to constantly forget this most necessary of operations.

Expert opinion varies on what action to take if you should happen to slip up. Some authorities say you can paint catalyst on to the surface of the resinglass and that this will cure up to two or three thicknesses of resinglass. Others doubt that such an action would have more than a surface effect. I do not know where the truth lies in this argument, but undoubtedly if you strip off any uncatalysed resinglass and throw it away you cannot go wrong. It is a costly and time-consuming remedy perhaps but I bet you only do it once.

I believe some people are allergic to resin, so they would obviously have to wear rubber gloves of some sort while doing resin work. We tried gloves at first but they were awkward and only lasted a day at the most before tearing.

Not having done manual work for some time our hands were soft and at first the resin stung, but after the first day we got used to it and it gave no further trouble. We always used Kerodex barrier cream before and Kerocleanse after resin work. Funnily we found that the Kerocleanse stung almost as much as the resin and brought soft forearms out in a rash, which fortunately disappeared after a few minutes (the rash not the forearms).

Once you have all the resin weighed out, and barrier cream rubbed into your hands, catalyse the first bucket of resin. This now has to be divided so that everybody has a bucket with some resin, and a brush.

Assuming that there are three of you, body number one brushes resin on to the foam while body number two unrolls the glass on to the resin before the latter has had a chance to run down the hull. The third person comes along behind, brushing more resin on to the cloth.

If your resin has a gelling time of thirty minutes you should find it possible to go on like this for about fifteen minutes, then prop up the roll of glass and all go back to the beginning again to dab on more resin where necessary and generally make sure the cloth is thoroughly wetted out and stretched as tightly as possible.

Obviously there should be no bubbles in the resinglass and, most important in sandwich construction, the foam should be saturated with resin to give the best possible bond between the skins and the core of the lamination.

It takes time for the resin to break down the binders used in the manufacture of the glass (it has to do this before it can penetrate the glass properly) so do not be too eager to start brushing extra resin on to the glass. In fact we found it made wetting out more difficult if we tried to work on the glass too soon after the resin had been put on. Put the glass and resin on and then leave well alone for five or ten minutes and the glass will almost wet itself out.

After three or four long lengths of cloth we were quite at home using resin and glass and found that, provided the number three in the team was prepared to work hard and keep his wits about him, numbers one and two could press on laying on resin and glass, stopping only to mix more resin as necessary while number three moved backwards and forwards between brushing resin on the newly-laid glass and putting the finishing touches to glass laid some time before.

This system can only work if the man working as number three is prepared to yell for help if he has the slightest suspicion that the resin is about to go off before he has had a chance to check on the wetting out. The resin we used seemed to have a short period just prior to actual gelling when it could still be worked but was showing signs of getting sticky.

Numbers one and two must do all the mixing of resin, brush washing, etc., and be prepared to help out immediately if called.

Working with 9 lb. batches of resin, if you get the system working well and your catalyst content right, you will probably find that, as numbers one and two are unrolling the twenty-seventh foot of glass, number three should be putting the final touches to the fifteenth foot of glass while the first nine feet are just starting to go off.

If out of every 9 lb. batch of resin you aim to put about 5 lb. under the glass and 3 lb. on top, leaving a pound for dabbing on later where necessary, you should not go far wrong.

Ideally of course the resin should be applied in a nice even coat, both under and on the glass. Mohair rollers are sometimes recommended for this but we found they went hard very easily and anyway $1\frac{1}{2}''$ or $2''$ brushes were just as convenient. If you do use mohair rollers you will still need brushes to stretch the cloth out.

When working on vertical or sloping surfaces aim to put more of the resin near the top rather than the bottom, especially under the glass. Not only will the resin run down a bit before you can unroll the glass on to it but the resin continues to drain down even after the glass has been put on.

Provided your resin-to-glass ratio is about right you should find that you can put glass along a quite vertical surface without it sliding off or curling over at the top.

The glass should be stretched as tight as you can get it within reason. We found it helped to tape the glass to the hull at the start with a few strips of masking tape. With a little care it was then possible for number three to finish his brushing out with a few hard strokes all in the one direction away from the fixed end. Be careful, especially until the first lot of resin has gone off, that the end of the cloth does not work along. Tape will not stick on wet resin, so put it on before you start with the resin.

If number two is unrolling the glass so that it is going on loosely in the first place, number three will find that he is trying to work a large amount of excess glass along. In this case it is a good idea for numbers one and two to go back and help out so that number three can concentrate on his main task of making sure that the glass is fully wetted out before the resin goes off.

As well as trying to get the glass on fairly tightly, number two has also to stop the roll of glass from taking charge. Woven roving is a very slippery, heavy sort of stuff and, working along a more or less vertical face, the inside of the roll is just waiting for an opportunity to slide out and cover the immediate landscape. Even when taped to a solid core of some sort, a ten-yard roll of woven roving bears a striking resemblance to a juicy orange pip between wet fingers.

This problem is not so great that complicated precautions are necessary, but number two should be aware of it and take the necessary measures before things get out of hand. We found it sufficient to hold the roll of glass at the very bottom with one hand, fingers going up the middle of the roll preferably, and with the other hand hold it at a point about two-thirds of the way up the roll.

A certain amount of resin will dribble down while you are doing the job, and there are bound to be splashes of resin on the foam. It these are allowed to gell into hard nibs and ridges they will be embarrassing when you come to put on your next piece of

17a. Eighteen-ounce undirectional woven roving that has just been unrolled on to wet resin. The masking tape used to stop the glass cloth from fraying can be seen along the cut edges.

b. About five minutes later, after resin has been brushed on top.

18a. Another five minutes and the masking tape is ready to come off. You can just see little streaks of unwetted glass.

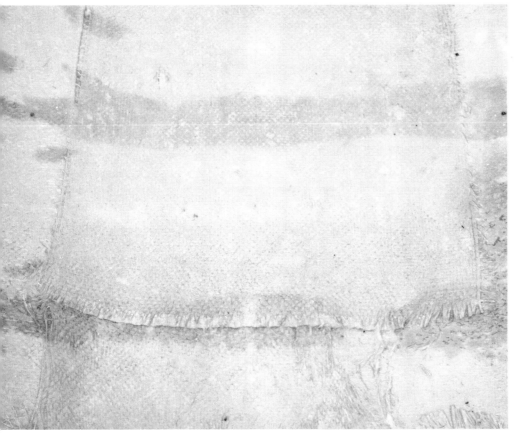

b. Fully wetted out and the edges flattened as much as possible. Towards the upper left-hand side you can see a bubble, this was caused by leaving a small nib on an earlier piece of resinglass.

glass, so keep your eyes open for stray blobs of resin and brush them well into the foam before they have a chance to harden.

The one place where the inexperienced amateur is likely to run into trouble with resinglass is with wetting out—not because the wetting out itself is terribly difficult or complicated but because without experience you do not know what to look for as an indication of the degree of wetting out. With a little experience it is easy to see at a glance whether a piece of glass is wetted out properly, but until you gain this experience you will have to examine the lay-up very closely.

At first when undirectional woven roving is unrolled on to wet resin it is white and very shiny. Then the resin applied on top of the glass starts to have its effect on the binders and the glass loses its white shiny appearance.

If you look at a length of glass about five minutes after the resin has been applied, the chances are you will see patches that are much whiter than the rest of the length. These areas are due to the uneven application of resin which is inevitable with hand lay-up. They must be given more resin (this is why I suggest that of a 9 lb. resin mix you put only 5 lb. under and 3 lb. on top of the glass, leaving a pound in hand for this job).

Examine the glass a few minutes later and you should see that practically all the glass has become indivisible and you can see the foam quite clearly through the wet resin glass. Look very closely, however, and the chances are you will see little bunches of glass strands in the centres of the rovings of the cloth. Although the strands in these bunches are not completely white, indicating that some resin is present, they are certainly not invisible as they should be. Generally all that is called for is a few strokes with the brush which works the resin right into the glass and the strands become invisible.

You will quickly learn to judge if a little brushing is all that is required or if another dab of resin is needed as well.

Once all the strands of glass have disappeared and the resinglass has become a transparent layer you can say thorough wetting out has been achieved.

Once the glass is wetted out you can check on the bond between resinglass and foam. If all the cells of the foam are full of resin the foam will appear a uniform pale golden colour under the wet resinglass. Areas of foam where the cells still contain air, rather than the strength-giving resin, will appear darker. The remedy is either more brushing or a dab more resin; experience will quickly tell you when more resin is necessary.

Chopped strand mat behaves and looks much the same as woven roving while it is being wetted out, except of course that the glass filaments run in all directions.

It is advisable to use a metal or plastic washer roller in the final stages of wetting out mat. It is possible to get mat to wet out simply by stippling it with a brush, but we found this took quite a lot of resin and it was much harder work than when we used a washer roller. So using a roller saves work, resin and weight and because of the higher glass-to-resin ratio gives a stronger laminate.

68

Do not try to use the roller until the resin has had a good chance to penetrate the cloth by itself or you will be making work for yourself. Just how much rolling you have to do will depend mainly on your resin-to-glass ratio. The more resin you use the less rolling you will have to do but more than 3 lb. of resin to each pound of glass gives a resin-rich laminate, while less than 2 lb. gives a resin-starved one.

Probably the sensible thing to do if you are not used to working in resinglass is to start off using 3 lb. of resin to one of glass and to either stick to this ratio or gradually cut down on the amount of resin as you gain experience and confidence.

When the professional moulders use mat they get one piece wetted out, then while it is still wet another piece is laid on top. This works all right with a resin-to-glass ratio of three to one, but with less resin than this it is not really satisfactory. With lower resin contents a certain amount of pressure is needed on the washer roller to get thorough wetting out, which is impossible unless you are rolling on a fairly firm surface. Because of this you will find it necessary where you have several layers of mat to give each layer time to go hard before putting on the next. Freshly-gelled resin makes new resin go off quickly, so allow a few hours between layers.

To get a good bond, fresh resinglass should not be put on top of other resinglass which is much more than twenty-four hours old unless the older resinglass is first scuffed up with a sander. We found with our second hull that we were organized and experienced enough to be able to make the complete hull without having to do any sanding except for the removal of nibs and whiskers along the seams.

I think organization and having a clear idea of what you are going to do are far more important than experience. Therefore have everything ready before you start and keep the hull fair and free from lumps and bumps as you go along.

A three-inch portable belt sander is quicker than a disc sander for scuffing up large areas but I do not think there is much in it.

Resinglass dust by the way is an irritant (we christened it prickle dust); it is so fine that protection against it is almost impossible—short of a space suit. Grinding off was undoubtedly the most unpleasant job of the summer so it is to be avoided whenever possible.

As we were working more or less in the open we did not use respirators while doing the bulk of the resinglass work. We did however wear them while doing resinglass work inside the completed shell, and we always wore them while glass dust was in the air from grinding off.

The number of layers and type of resinglass you need on the outside of your boat will depend on what sort of craft she is and on her size. Derek Kelsall has found that he gets a strong light-weight structure by using layers of 18 oz. unidirectional woven roving so that the glass strands run first along the hull, decks, etc., then across, then along, and so on until the required thickness is reached, rather like plywood.

Our boat is lightly skinned, just two layers of 18 oz. unidirectional woven roving inside and out with further reinforcing along the keel. A mono-hull using the weight of a heavy-ballast keel and large sail area to drive itself through the water might need more than this.

The surest way of finding out how much resinglass any particular design will need is to approach a naval architect who has practical experience in using P.V.C. foam sandwich, and get him to advise on structural details, e.g. skin thickness, bulkheads, etc.

Unidirectional woven roving is not overlapped at the edges but is butt-joined like wall paper. Therefore there are no extra thicknesses of resinglass to make life difficult at the finishing stage.

Unidirectional woven roving can only be laid on a fairly smooth surface. If you try to lay unidirectional cloth over a blob or nib of hardened resin you will find the cloth lifts up to leave a large bubble, on the bell-tent principle, which is obviously not very good. All hardened resinglass must be checked over and nibs, blobs, etc., ground off before fresh resinglass is put on top. Especially check the seams between two lengths of

19. Two layers of 18 oz. undirectional woven roving in place with some extra reinforcing at the bottom of the transom.

20. Running the Grinderette over the joints between two pieces of cloth to remove any hard whiskers of resinglass before putting on the second layer of resinglass.

unidirectional cloth; little whiskers of glass tend to stand up along them which play havoc with new resinglass.

Seams also tend to contain a row of bubbles and these should be filled with resin putty before new resinglass is put on top.

We found glass varied from roll to roll. One roll would go down quite smoothly, leaving practically no bits to be ground off, while another would 'pick-up' all over the place and leave quite a number of little bumps of resinglass to be ground off.

In the notes that follow I shall be dealing solely with unidirectional woven roving; when I refer to 'longitudinal pieces' of layers I shall be referring to the glass cloth whose rovings run along the length of the hull. Cloth whose rovings run round the hull I shall call 'transverse pieces'.

You can start putting on the longitudinal lengths of cloth either at the gunwale or keel, it is not important, just as long as the cloth is running more or less along the hull and not tending to 'corkscrew' off too badly. We started at the gunwale and did some cutting at the keel and bow to stop the glass running off. Remember to brush out any runs or splashes of resin before they have a chance to harden, otherwise you will have the trouble of grinding them off later.

Because of their length and the semi-vertical nature of boat topsides, these longitudinal lengths of cloth are the most awkward to put on. Anyone working solo might find it easier to work in short pieces rather than to attempt the full length of the hull in one go. Short pieces should really be as long as you can handle and certainly no shorter than about ten feet.

To give the same strength as a single length of cloth, even though it has been cut into three or four pieces, each piece must overlap the preceding one by about four inches. To do this effectively you must allow the first piece of resinglass to go hard. Then the end can be feathered back with a disc sander before fresh resinglass is laid on top, otherwise you will get a line of air bubbles across the joint—this is not to be recommended (Fig. 15).

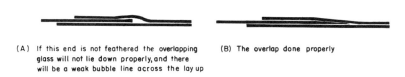

(A) If this end is not feathered the overlapping glass will not lie down properly, and there will be a weak bubble line across the lay up

(B) The overlap done properly

Fig. 15.   Ends of resinglass must be feathered before more glass is laid on top.

The transverse lengths of glass should offer no problems. Start in the middle and work towards the ends of the hull.

If there are at least two of you, the transverse cloth can be run from gunwale to gunwale. But rather than to try to work up one side then down the other it is easier to put the glass on two rollers, start at the keel, and work down both sides simultaneously. Anyone working solo would find it easier to use separate lengths of cloth for each side and give them a good overlap along the keel. No matter how many people are working, eventually as you work towards the bow you will find it impossible to run glass right over the hull without getting overlaps along the edge. It is better to cut the glass and have a good overlap along the keel where the extra thickness of glass can do the most good. But the end of the first piece of cloth must be feathered back in each case.

Be very careful where the cloth goes round an inside angle or radius, e.g. at the keel-hull junction, along knuckle lines, etc. The cloth will tend to pull away from such places as you stretch it. So when the cloth is fully wetted out, but before the resin has started to go off, stipple along all inside curves with a brush to make sure there are no bubbles under the resinglass.

It is possible to use the same brush for putting on four or five batches of resin. But there is a possibility of contaminating the new mix of resin with so much older resin that the new mix gels much faster than it should. This is not only expensive on brushes but it is more than possible that the resin will go off before you have had a chance to wet out the glass thoroughly. We changed brushes and buckets after two 9 lb. mixes of resin.

Usually number one in the team went to mix the new batch of resin while numbers two and three carried on wetting out the glass. Number one brought the fresh resin round in clean buckets with clean brushes for everyone. At the same time he collected the dirty buckets and brushes. The dirty buckets were left so that the dregs of resin could harden, while the brushes were washed thoroughly in acetone.

It is quite easy to break the hardened resin out of the plastic buckets when they are needed again. Using about a dozen buckets we found we only needed bucket-cleaning sessions first thing in the morning and immediately after lunch.

Acetone is absolutely essential if you are going to do any amount of resin work. Initially we had a lot of trouble organizing a supply of the stuff, and I let the man in the paint shop sell me a couple of gallons of brush cleaner; it was worse than useless. Chemists can get acetone for you but it takes time and it is rather expensive. Eventually we hit upon the idea of trying our local professional moulders. One of them was quite happy to sell acetone to us, at a fraction of the chemist's price, provided we took our own tin and collected it. He also sold us chopped strand mat cheaper than we could get is elsewhere.

We kept a few pints of acetone in a couple of buckets for brush washing. It evaporates very quickly so the containers must be covered; we used scrap foam with a brick on top.

It is no good just putting resin-filled brushes into acetone—the resin goes off just the same rendering the brushes useless. Excess resin should be squeezed out of the brush, then the brush must be worked up and down vigorously in acetone so that the acetone gets right into the bristles.

We used two buckets of acetone. The first wash was used to get most of the resin out of the brush, which was then simply left standing in the more or less clean acetone of the second bucket until needed again. After a while the first wash starts to get thick with resin; (if left long enough it will in fact go quite hard, along with any brushes left in it). It should be thrown away and replaced with clean acetone, which then becomes the second wash while the other bucket of slightly dirty acetone becomes the first wash.

In our first four days of doing resin work we lost nearly a dozen brushes and six mohair rollers, either because we had no acetone or because we left brushes overnight in thick acetone which had gone hard by the morning. Not only did the second dozen brushes do for the resin work on the rest of the boat, but we still have three completely unused.

Any sort of electric disc sander can be used for grinding off nibs and blobs of hardened resin, but undoubtedly the best tool is the Wolf Grinderette. It is very light, so it is not as tiring to use as a seven-inch angle grinder, yet because it revolves so quickly it is as fast to use.

RESIN: SPECIAL CONSIDERATIONS

Foam sandwich hulls must be protected along the bottom for when they take the ground. Mono-hulls will of course have some sort of ballast keel. Multi-hulls need some sort of skeg to sit on.

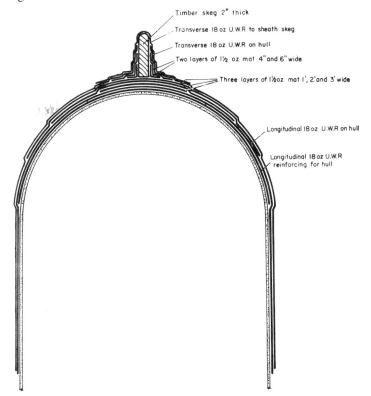

Timber skeg 2" thick
Transverse 18 oz U.W.R to sheath skeg
Transverse 18 oz U.W.R on hull
Two layers of 1½ oz mat 4" and 6" wide
Three layers of 1½oz mat 1', 2'and 3' wide
Longitudinal 18 oz U.W.R on hull
Longitudinal 18 oz U.W.R reinforcing for hull

Fig. 16. Lay up and skeg attachment to our 40-foot catamaran. Reading from the bottom gives the order in which the various layers of resinglass were applied.

The skegs on our catamaran are of oak, two inches thick, and they are about ten feet long. Four layers of resinglass were used to attach them to the hulls (Fig. 16). Wooden skegs are quick and easy, if you can get them cut on a band saw (Sandwich Marina supplied ours ready shaped). Otherwise it might be easier, and very nearly as cheap, to make resinglass skegs using low-density polyurethane foam as a core.

Resinglass skegs need wooden or metal shoes to protect them from abrasion, but these can simply be screwed and resinglassed in place, so they are no problem.

Ballast keels are more complicated, though nothing to be frightened of. Either they can be of hollow resinglass into which ballast is placed, or, if the design is extreme fin and bulb type, a metal fin can be bolted to the hull and the ballast bolted to that.

The metal fin keel is quite straightforward. Your designer should give construction details, and details of any hull reinforcing that may be necessary. To keep as much strain off the hull as possible until the resinglass has had a good chance to cure, and to make it easier for one to climb in and out of the boat, it is a good idea to leave the mating of hull and fin as long as possible. It could in fact be left almost until the boat is ready for the water.

The fin must of course be a good fit to the hull. The easiest way to ensure this, assuming it is fairly close anyway, is to have a couple of layers of wet resinglass (chopped strand mat) between the fin and hull when they are bolted together.

The metal can be faired up to a good aerofoil shape and thickness by sticking low-density polyurethane foam on either side and then covering the whole thing with a couple of layers of resinglass. Remember to make some provision for inspecting the keel bolts, even if it is only a little patch of resinglass that you can tear off and replace after the inspection.

21.   Low-density polyurethane foam covered with mat was used for the skeg of the dinghy.

There are two methods of making keels or bilge keels in which the ballast is encapsulated.

The first method is only suitable for craft with wide, shallow keels, of the older sort of design in which the keel is very much a part of the hull rather than a fin stuck on a dish. (That is not intended as a criticism of modern design, I just could not think of a better description.)

When constructing one of these older type of boats, it is possible to make up the complete hull, including keel, at the mould and foam stages. The keel is heavily resinglassed. Then, after the hull has been taken off the mould, the foam can be cut away from where the ballast is going to be placed and the inside of the keel resinglassed. This is a quick, simple method, especially if you cover the foam that has to be removed with a piece of aluminium foil before you put any resinglass on the outside of the hull.

The semi-fin keel is the most complicated to make but even this should offer no real problems. It is possible to make up a fin on a former using two or three layers of resinglass; bond this to the foam of the hull, fair it up with foam and resin putty, then add further layers of resinglass until the fin is of the required thickness. The main snag with this method is in ensuring that the fin is properly lined up with the hull.

A much better and easier method is to build up the fin from hardboard and soft wood in position on the hull mould, before putting on the foam (Fig. 17). If the whole thing is covered with aluminium foil and then waxed the resinglass should release easily. Cover any joints in the foil with masking tape, which will stop resin finding its way into the mould to stick everything firmly together.

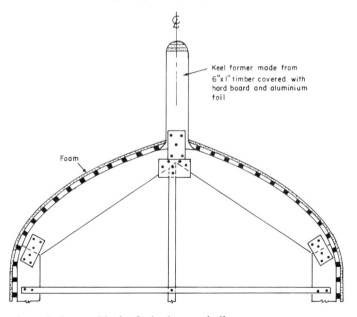

Fig. 17. Section through the mould of a fin keel mono-hull.

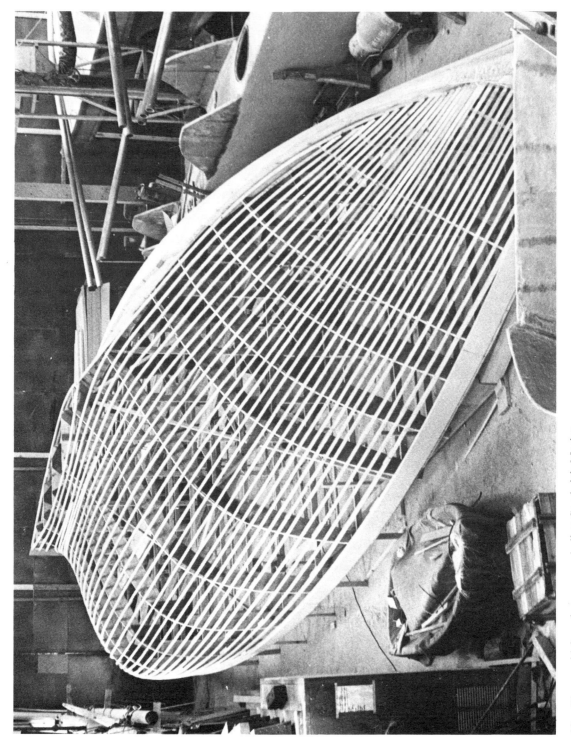

22.   The mould for a large mono-hull at Sandwich Marina.

Bilge keels can be made in exactly the same way. But if they are splayed out at all the keel formers will have to be made so that they stay in the hull when it is lifted off the mould. They can then be withdrawn individually.

If your fin has a ballast bulb at the bottom, you will have to make the former so that it can be broken out from inside the fin. In fact it is probably a good idea to use nails rather than screws in the construction of any fin former, so that it is easy to break out if it refuses to pull in one piece.

Finishing

Resinglass needs a coating of some sort to protect it from water. In a normal moulded hull the gell coat provides this protection and it is possible to brush gell coat or resin on to the outside of a foam-sandwich hull. This, however, does not fill up the weave of the glass fabric and generally it gives a poor finish.

It is far better to use trowelling cement, or a stiff resin putty.

Aim to put the putty on so that it fills the weave of the resinglass and makes a coat of resin putty about $\frac{1}{32}''$ thick on the outside of the hull. Once the putty has gone hard

23. Putting on the resin putty with a plasterer's float. As you can see I need a lot of practice.

24. Using the finishing sander. The grim expression was because we had to move the dinghy from the boat club and I forgot to take my respirator home.

the hull can be sanded to a smooth finish with an orbital sander and 40-grit paper. Slight hollows in the hull due to an unfair mould or different thicknesses of foam can be faired out with further local applications of resin putty.

For ease and quickness the finishing should be done while the hull is still upside down on the mould. In this case resin putty should not be put within six or seven inches of the gunwhale. The decks have to be bonded to the hull in this area, and it is much stronger to bond on to the resinglass of the hull rather than to a layer of resin putty.

We did not start making our boat until near the end of July. As work progressed and time was wasted on the first hull working out how to do things, it became obvious that we could not spend time doing finishing work and still have the boat weatherproof by the first frost. So we took our hulls off the mould before we had done any finishing work at all. The finishing has since been done with the hulls up the right way with all the decks and cabins on. It was a little difficult and it was obvious that it would have been much, much easier if we could have done the job while the hulls were upside down on the mould.

Fillers vary considerably in hardness and price. For the job it has to do on a foam sandwich boat the softest, cheapest talc filler you can get is good enough. Hard fillers like the French B.L.R. give an excellent finish, but they are heavy and terribly difficult to sand down. This is not very important on something the size of a dinghy, but on anything bigger a filler which gives adequate protection with the minimum of effort is called for.

The filler powder is mixed with resin to a stiff paste, catalysed, then applied with a metal plasterer's float which has had all its corners and edges filed round.

It is quicker if there are two of you for this job. One person to mix and catalyse the filler, while the other puts it on the hull. A few experiments will show how much filler you need for each pound of resin. Ideally the filler mixture should be fluid enough to trowel on easily, yet stiff enough to stay where put, and not run down the hull.

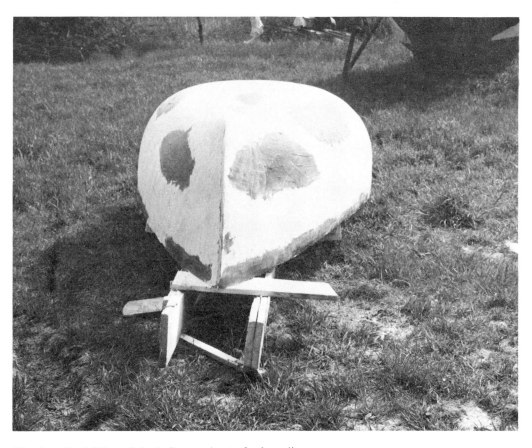

25.   Localized filling of the hollows prior to final sanding.

26. Using the disc grinder to smooth out the worst of the bumps in the filler.

Using our materials we found 1½ lb. of filler powder in 1 lb. of resin was just about right, and this quantity was sufficient to cover about nine square feet of hull. If the resin putty is too fluid you will find it very difficult to get a smooth result.

It is important that the catalyst is mixed into the resin putty well, otherwise you are liable to find soft patches on the hull which have to be scraped off and redone. We found it easiest if we put half the required amount of filler powder into the resin, added the catalyst, then stirred the mix very well before adding the remainder of the filler powder. This could only be done immediately before use of course.

There is a knack to plastering the outside of a hull and I must admit I have not got it. You will find you make a better job, however, if you work from left to right, assuming that you are right handed, work up and over the hull rather than down or along, apply the filler in small quantities (about half a cupful) with the left-hand half of your float, and do not press too hard. Experiment holding the float at different angles until you get something like a smooth result. If you are as much of a rabbit at

82

plastering as I was you will have to smooth your hardened filler initially with a Grinderette using 60-grit discs before using the orbital sander.

When the hull comes off the mould and is turned up the right way it needs some sort of cradle to sit in. This should be made and fitted while the hull is on the mould. The cradle needs to be strong enough to hold the hull without it moving while you move around putting resinglass on the inside. We did not have a fin keel on our hull to worry about, so a simple frame made from 6″ × 1″ at either end of the skeg was all we needed. A similar sized monohull would need a cradle made from 4″ × 2″ and 6″ × 1″ timber.

Do not forget that until you get the sandwich completed, by putting resinglass on the inside, your hull will be quite flexible and it will distort easily. So give it all the support you can and use plywood pads to spread the load as much as possible.

It is a good idea to make up a few braces to fit across the hull and hold it in shape at the gunwale. These can be made from 2″ × 1″ with scraps of ply screwed to either end. Put one about every four feet along the hull. They can all be made up from measurements taken while the hull is still on the mould but remember to mark both them and their positions on the hull to avoid any possibility of error.

At this stage the hull will tend to flop outwards, so it is necessary to have pieces of plywood only on the outsides of the braces. After the resinglass has been put on the inside of the hull, the hull will tend to curl in at the gunwale. Then further pieces of ply will be added to the braces, but if these inside pieces of ply are added now you will find they get in the way when you are putting on the resinglass (Fig. 18).

Go round inside the mould and mark the frame positions and bulkhead positions on the foam. The bulkhead positions should already be marked on the stringers of the mould (see Ch. 1) and there is no problem in marking the foam in the right place with a pencil.

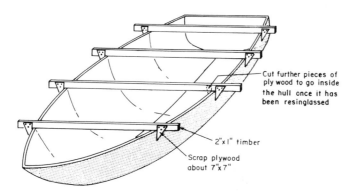

Cut further pieces of ply wood to go inside the hull once it has been resinglassed

2″x1″ timber

Scrap plywood about 7″x7″

Fig. 18. Cut braces ready to fit across the hull to hold the gunwales in shape while the inside is resinglassed.

The frame positions are a little more difficult to mark because of the gap between the edge of the frame and the foam caused by the stringers. In the end we held a pencil flat against the face of the mould frame and marked the foam with that. This meant the lines were about one-eighth of an inch out of position but we allowed for this when we needed the frame positions while making the decks. The centre line can also be drawn down the keel.

It is nice to have some idea where the water line is inside the boat when it comes to fitting out so mark it in with a pencil while you are marking everything else.

Bulkheads should be made now so that they are ready to put in as soon as the inside of the hull has been resinglassed. Making them now also gives the resinglass on the outside of the hull more time to cure. And if two or three of you are working together one person can get on using the orbital sander while the others get on with the wood-work; this way you only need one orbital sander.

The position and construction of bulkheads is something for your designer. We have three bulkheads in our hulls. The main one is of box construction, 8 mm. marine ply on a 1″-thick red cedar and mahogany frame. The bulkhead at the forward end of the cockpit is 18 mm. marine ply, while there is an 8 mm. marine-ply bulkhead forward of the accommodation.

In addition to these we have two box beams of 8 mm. marine ply on $3'' \times 1\frac{1}{2}''$ mahogany frames and two alloy beams, but these beams are to hold the hulls together and are not necessary on mono-hull craft.

Resinglass does not bond very well to wood and for this reason it is a good idea to drill a series of holes round the edges of bulkheads, then the resinglass that is used to bond the bulkhead to the hull can be worked into the holes giving a good mechanical bond. We drilled 1″ diameter holes, five inches apart and one and a half inches in from the edge all round our bulkheads. If you have box construction bulkheads do not drill through the frame timber, just drill the plywood.

A carpenter's brace with an auger bit can be used to make these holes, but we found we spent more time swearing and clearing the bit than actually drilling. After various experiments we found the best thing was a hole saw used in a good powerful electric drill. You can get by for a few holes with a small domestic type electric drill, but you have to be careful not to overload it. It is much quicker if you are building any size of boat to hire or borrow a decent-sized drill.

The bulkheads we found were no problem. We hired a portable jig saw for a few days to do all the cutting, so there was no back ache there. Even in the box bulkhead the strength is in the plywood rather than the timber frame so no fancy joints were called for. It was simply a matter of glueing $1\frac{1}{2}'' \times 1''$ timber to the plywood in the appropriate place with marine glue, then hammering in several bronze grip-fast nails to hold the joint while the glue set; these would also act as a line of reserve just in case the glue should fail. When the glue had dried, plywood was glued and nailed to the other side of the $1\frac{1}{2}'' \times 1''$ frame.

85

27.   John and Mike working on the support for
our first hull.

Tests on offcuts showed that the timber fractured before the glue line, which I must admit I found not only pleasing but rather amazing and I am still not sure I believe it.

Bulkheads for a mono-hull and trimaran will be made in one piece. This however is not practical with a catamaran. The box beams for a catamaran should be made in one piece but you will find it easier if you make the bulkheads in three pieces (Fig. 19). Then you can put the hull part of the bulkhead in position as soon as the inside skin of resinglass has been put in the hull, and join the hulls with the centre section when everything has been lined up. Where the different parts of the bulkhead join put butt

28. Looking aft in our starboard hull before the bulkheads had been bonded in place. The pieces of mat used to tack the bulkhead in place show clearly.

straps, on one side only, until everything is finally in place between the hulls. These give you something to clamp to without hiding the joint.

To make the strongest possible joint where two pieces of plywood have to be joined put a ply butt strap on both sides of the joint. These should be glued and nailed with grip-fast nails. Not only are such joints strong, but they do away with the necessity for scarfing. The 8 mm. butt straps we made eight inches wide, while the 18 mm. ones were ten inches wide.

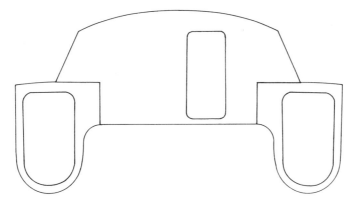

Fig. 19. Typical catamaran bulkhead made in three pieces. The two outer pieces should be positioned temporarily in the hulls as soon as the inner resinglass skin has gelled. The centre section is fixed into place once the hulls have been lined up and the bridge deck cut to size.

If your equipment is capable of it a neater job can be made of the butt straps if their edges are cut at an angle—45 degrees is ideal. Unfortunately our saw would only work at 90 degrees, but the result was not too bad. Eventually we shall probably put fillets by the butt straps to give the same effect as a chamfered edge.

Until the inner resinglass is put on the hull is quite flexible, and some sort of internal support is necessary when it is rolled over. The mould of course is ideal, but this is not very practical if you are planning to re-use it. If you are planning to lift the hull off the mould, so that the latter can be used again, have some fairly substantial pieces of timber (4″ × 2″ should be about right) ready to wedge between the gunwales before you roll the hull up the right way.

The final preparation before taking the hull off the mould is to undo all the screws holding the foam to the mould. This is a rather tedious job, made doubly so by the exciting thoughts of being so near to seeing what it really looks like the right way up. Pump screwdrivers are no good for this job, but we found that we could put the bit from the pump screwdriver into a wheel brace. This combination was much faster than an ordinary screwdriver.

No doubt you will miss the odd screw or two, but they should not make much difference when you come to lift the hull off the mould or break the mould out of the hull.

29.   Ready to break out the mould, the strong back has already gone.

Once preparations are complete the hull and mould can be parted.

The hull can be lifted off the mould with a crane or tackle, and then rolled up the right way. Or the mould and hull can be rolled over together and the mould lifted or broken out of the hull.

If you are going to use the mould again and do not want the bother of remaking it you will have to lift the hull off the mould before turning it up the right way. With a catamaran or trimaran it is a simple matter to drill a couple of one-inch holes through the wooden skeg and pass a rope through these and over the hook of a small crane. How you lift a mono-hull will depend both on the design and on you. Ring bolts can be put through the keel temporarily, in which case pieces of plywood would be needed on the inside of the hull to spread the load. Or four metal plates could be turned under the gunwale to make hooks and the hull lifted by these.

At this stage even quite a large hull will weigh only a few hundred pounds, so ring bolts, or any other aid for lifting which you adopt, do not have to be fantastically strong.

Once it is off the mould keep the hull upside down while you wedge three or four pieces of 4″ × 2″ across the hull at its widest part. Use ply pads on the ends to spread the load as much as possible. Without these struts the hull will tend to collapse when you roll it on to its side and it is just possible that the bond between resinglass and foam could be broken somewhere.

Once the inside struts are in place it is quite easy for three or four men to roll the hull over so that it is up the right way supported by its cradle.

In this state the hull could quite easily be twisted, so remove the internal struts and put the prepared lengths of 2″ × 1″ across the gunwales, (these should have all been measured and marked while the hull was still on the mould). Mark the centres of these braces with a pencil line. Now it is simply a matter of using a plumb bob to check that the centres of the braces are exactly over the centre line, which you should have drawn along the keel while the hull was still on the mould.

The cradle can be packed up where necessary until the hull is true.

Use plenty of struts on the hull so that it is quite firm. You will be walking about

30. Two large trimaran floats at Sandwich Marina. The simple timber supports show clearly.

inside to put the inner resinglass skin on and you do not want the whole thing wobbling about under you, possibly acquiring a permanent twist.

If you do not want to re-use the mould or you cannot get or afford a crane to lift your hull off, roll the hull over with the mould still inside.

The strong back is rather an embarrassment when doing this job, so undo all the screws holding the frames, stem and stern to it. Be careful that the hull and mould do not slip off the strong back and hurt someone's foot. In fact the safest thing is to lift the hull and mould, still upside down, away from the strong back completely. If you carry first one end a foot or two, and then the other, you will be surprised how few people it takes to do the job.

The hull and mould can now be rolled over so that they are up the right way. Check that the hull is not twisted and pack the cradle if necessary. Wedge the cradle and prop the hull so that it is completely firm, even when you move around inside the hull.

Remove the mould either by lifting it out in one piece or by breaking it out piecemeal with a heavy hammer. If you do break the mould out try to remember that the foam dents easily and that you will have to fill the dents up with resin putty before you put on any resinglass.

31. The support is not really necessary on a craft this size, but it helps to keep everything still while putting on the inner skin of resinglass. The struts across at the gunwales are especially important on craft with flat topsides.

Inside the Hull

The inside of the hull quickly gets dirty if you are not careful, therefore it is a good idea to have a pair of clean shoes which are changed before you climb out of the hull. As the foam is soft and dents easily before the first layer of resinglass is put on it helps if the shoes are of soft canvas and rubber though even these leave heel marks if you are heavy footed.

The order of working is much the same as for doing the outside of the hull. Fair up the hull with resin putty; cut out foam and replace with resinglass where necessary; put on required thickness of resinglass; bond in bulkheads and ballast.

The holes made by the screws used to hold the foam to the mould do not need filling with resin putty. They are quite small and resin will run in and fill them up at the resinglass stage.

Seams between pieces of foam will need filling, however, and so will any dents or largish holes caused by screws being torn out of the foam. Hard angles in the foam, e.g. at the opening at the top of a ballast keel, must be softened to a radius of half an inch or so.

Derek Kelsall recommends that the foam at the bow should be cut out and replaced by solid resinglass (Fig. 20). He does however admit that some boats have not had this treatment and they do not appear to have suffered.

If you have built a ballast keel from foam integral with the hull it will be necessary to cut the foam away where the ballast is going to rest. Otherwise the foam will slowly compress and after a time your ballast will start to move, eventually wear a hole in the bottom of the boat and fall out, which I imagine could be rather embarrassing.

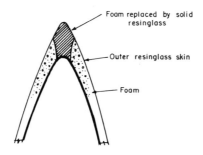

Fig. 20. Section through bow showing foam cut away and replaced by solid resinglass before inner skin of resinglass is put on hull.

32. This is what the inside looks like after the mould has been removed and the seams filled. The screw holes fill up with resin when the inner skin of resinglass is put on.

On a mono-hull it may also be necessary to replace some of the foam with solid resinglass in the keel area, but your designer will tell you if and where this is necessary.

When it comes to putting on the resinglass make sure you take everything into the hull that you are going to need before you start. Not only is it a nuisance having to climb out to get an extra drop of resin or a knife, it is virtually impossible to change shoes with hands covered in resin, so you keep on your boat shoes and dirt gets carried into the hull.

The easiest way to work is from the ends towards the middle. It is possible to put some of the longitudinal lengths of glass on in one piece. But we found it easier to use two pieces with an overlap of six inches or so.

To put down the reinforcing length of resinglass that runs along the bottom of our hull we started from the stern with a piece of glass nine feet long. Because of the curve of the hull the glass was not rolled on a cardboard core.

33. A 60-foot ketch building at Sandwich Marina, showing an alternative to cutting the foam away at the bow. The mould has been built up to the foam line in the appropriate place and covered with polythene. The outer layers of resinglass will be taken over the polythene, then, after the hull has been lifted off the mould, extra layers of resinglass will be added inside.

Two people worked inside the hull unrolling the glass on to the resin and putting more resin on top of the glass in the normal way. The resin tends to run down the hull and form a patch of resin-rich lay up in the bottom of the hull, so try to put the bulk of the first application of resin up the sides of the hull rather than on the bottom. The third member of our team stood on a ladder outside the hull and, with a brush taped to a piece of stick, dabbed more resin on where necessary and saw to the final wetting out.

The two people in the hull then started with the other piece of cloth at the bow, working towards the stern. By the time that piece of cloth had been more or less laid, the resinglass laid in the stern had gone off so that the end could be feathered off with a disc sander and the people inside the hull could stand on it to lay the last of the second piece of cloth.

If when you are getting towards the end of the second piece of glass you find that the first piece has not gone off, you can wedge a plank across the hull and stand on that. You will not be able to feather the end of the first piece but, provided it really has not started to go off, the weight of the second piece of cloth and some heavy stippling with a brush will flatten it so that it does not form a ridge in the second piece of resinglass. Something is probably wrong with your catalyst if this happens, and some heat is called for to accelerate the curing of the resin, unless of course you are incredibly fast workers.

It is possible to rig up a plank along the bottom of the hull, on blocks, and stand on this to put the transverse pieces of glass on in one length from gunwale to gunwale going under the plank you are standing on. But we found it much easier to put the glass on in two pieces with a good overlap in the bottom of the boat.

Two people are best for this job, a third gets in the way. Tape the glass to the gunwale before you start, otherwise it will work down the hull under its own weight and the brushing it receives.

The bow section of a multi-hull is likely to be very narrow for working in. The only answer we found for this was for one man to work on his own, using two-foot-wide strips of glass instead of the usual four-foot-wide ones.

Depending on the make of resin you are using you may find your pencil marks starting to disappear after the second or third layer of resinglass, due to the colour of the resin. If this does occur it is a good idea to pencil the lines in again.

The resinglass in our hulls was completed with ten-inch-wide strips of chopped strand mat to reinforce the bulkhead positions. But your design may not need them.

As the resinglass cures inside the hull it will shrink and pull the hull in at the top (Fig. 21). Catamarans with large flat topsides suffer more in this respect than mono-hulls with plenty of curves. As soon as all the resinglass is on the inside of the hull, put the bulkheads in place—even if they are only tacked in place with a few small pieces of chopped strand mat they will hold the hull in shape—and brace between the gunwales every three or four feet with timber.

94

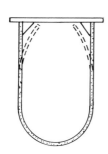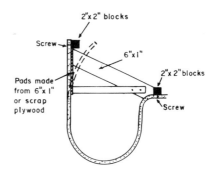

Fig. 21. Catamaran centre section bracing. Resinglass shrinks as it cures, and unless a hull is braced across at the gunwale it will distort, as shown by the dotted lines. The more there are of these braces the better, especially on catamaran hulls.

For ease of fitting the bulkheads want to be on the small side, say an eighth of an inch small all round. Four or five small wedges can then be used to hold the bulkhead in position on its marks while it is tacked in place with a few small pieces of chopped strand mat.

Once the bulkhead is firmly tacked in place it can be bonded in properly with its full quota of resinglass. Our design called for three layers of chopped strand mat— six, eight and ten inches wide—on both sides of all bulkheads. There is no reason, however, why the main bonding of the bulkheads should not wait until the decks and coach roof are all on and the hull is fully weathertight. This latter system is the one we adopted, and I think it makes sense for anyone working under a temporary shelter to do the same.

Encapsulated ballast in resinglass boats is almost a subject in its own right and your designer will be in a much better position to advise on this than I. But whatever ballast is used it must be rigidly fixed without any possibility of moving.

Scrap metal set in concrete is a cheap ballast, and is used by some professional moulders. Unfortunately substances leach out of concrete and attack the glass in a resinglass lay up. I would think it should be possible to line the inside of a fin keel with a thin sheet of polythene, and then pour in a metal concrete mix in thin layers, say four inches thick, with pieces of polythene between each layer. These could then be lifted out as soon as they had gone hard, (metal handles could be moulded in to help in this), and put on one side to dry. To seal the concrete they could be painted with three good coats of coal-tar epoxy compound, and given a fourth coat just prior to being placed permanently in the keel.

Before putting on the decks, or even setting the temporary deck supports in place, it is a good idea to scuff up the resinglass that you know is going to have things bonded to it, e.g. along the inside and outside of the gunwale where the decks will be bonded, and where the bulkhead bonding will be, though this latter is more easily done before the bulkheads are tacked into place.

34. Polyurethane foam was used to make this bulkhead. The wedges holding the bulkhead in place were removed when the tacking pieces of mat had gone hard.

SPECIAL CONSIDERATIONS

If you are making a catamaran, once the inside of the first hull is finished return to square one and start all over again.

When you have two hulls complete they must be lined up. This is not a terribly difficult job even in the middle of a rough field. Two men with a few rollers and a couple of thick pieces of wood for levers can move a forty-foot sandwich catamaran hull without any bother at all.

We used a spirit level to level up the hulls and then measured at bow and stern to make sure that they were parallel. The final check was to measure diagonally between bows and sterns.

The only problem we came up against was finding a tape measure that was reliable over forty-odd feet. It seemed daft to go and buy a steel tape just for half a day's use and the only one we could borrow was a linen one that stretched like tripe over this

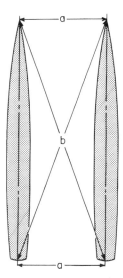

Fig. 22.   When lining up a pair of catamaran hulls both 'a' measurements should be the same, and so should the 'b'.

distance. In the end we hit upon the idea of employing the spring used for weighing resin to give us a constant tension (Fig. 23). This worked very well indeed: a few tests showed that, provided we kept the tension constant at nine pounds, we would not be more than $\frac{1}{32}''$ out. Now I do not know about you, but I am not going to let $\frac{1}{32}''$ in forty feet worry me.

Once the hulls are complete it is time to make the bridge deck. This can be made in one long piece but it will be rather heavy, especially if you are working short handed. We made ours in two pieces. One piece was the long, flat section, the curved front portion being the other.

To make the flat section first make a temporary floor from some sheets of plywood. Cover this with polythene, then lay out sheets of 18 mm. foam to make a piece the size

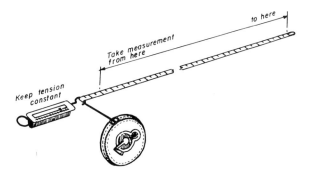

Fig. 23.   Using a linen tape to get reasonably accurate measurements over long distances.

of your bridge deck. The foam may curl up at the edges a little; if so put some nails through the foam into the plywood, leaving nearly half an inch of nail sticking out of the foam. Fill any poorly-fitting joints with resin putty and put on one layer of resinglass. The glass can be pulled down over the nails and stretched in the normal way.

When this has gelled pull all the nails out and give it a second layer of resinglass with the cloth running at right angles to the first layer.

Leave overnight to cure; then the thing, which will probably be getting quite heavy by this time, can be turned over. Two layers of resinglass are now applied to the other side. It is incredibly easy putting resinglass on a flat horizontal surface after working on a curved sloping hull.

When complete the bridge deck has to be lifted into place between the hulls. This was heavy work, for us, as there were only two of us working by that time. We managed by lifting up first one side and then the other, using trestles and props to support it until the final couple of lifts when it was supported by the fillets on either hull. We could not resist the temptation to have a quick walk on it, dreaming of cabins, masts and things.

With the bridge deck resting on the hull fillets run a pencil along the edge of the fillet underneath to give a cutting line. Then the whole thing can be taken down, dragged out of the way and turned over. It is then possible to cut the bridge deck to size—we used an ordinary cross-cut wood saw. Tend to cut the deck on the small side, and you will find it easier to fit later.

Stiffening ribs will be needed along the underside of the bridge deck. These are made from lengths of 4″ × 2″ low-density rigid polyurethane foam, covered with two layers of chopped strand mat about twelve and fourteen inches wide. These ribs, four in our case, can be put on when the bridge deck is in place, but the job is much easier and quicker if it is done while the bridge deck is still on the ground.

That piece of deck can be left to cure while the curved front part of the bridge deck is made. For this a mould is made in exactly the same way as the hull mould except that the stringers only need be about eighteen inches apart. Enough 18 mm. foam is laid out to cover this mould and given one layer of resinglass. After the resinglass has gone off the foam is screwed to the mould, resinglass-side down. The screws go into resinglass, and the mould has no great curve anyway, so it does not need many screws to hold the foam in place.

The top side is now given the required amount of resinglass and stiffeners to match those on the other part of the bridge deck.

When the bridge deck is ready the centre sections of the bulkheads and the two transverse beams can be lifted into place between the hulls and secured. Apart from the fact that our beams were on the heavy side the job was just about as easy as it sounds.

All that remains is to lift the bridge deck into place and prop it up while you fair in the joint between deck and fillet with resin putty and cover the joint with two layers of chopped strand mat to hold everything in place. The curved part at the front of the bridge deck can be offered up, marked, cut and fitted in exactly the same way.

If your design calls for a curved part at the back of the cockpit it can be made on the fillet mould, and put in place once the rest of the bridge deck has been finished. As time was running out this was not made and fitted until the following spring in our case.

Decks

After making the hull, the decks and coach roof are very quick and easy. Working entirely alone I made all the decks and superstructure of our catamaran in 200 hours, and believe me there is a lot of deck on a 40′ catamaran.

Basically the method of working is this. Using soft wood, erect a temporary support (which we called the form work) for the deck and coach roof; make up foam panels slightly oversize; resinglass these, on one side only, flat on the ground; put the pre-resinglassed panels in place on the form work, resinglass-side down; resinglass the upper side of the panels; resinglass all joints.

All the foam will be pre-resinglassed on one side and, as decks, etc., do not usually have any tight curves, the form work does not have to be very elaborate. A piece of shaped 6″ × 1″ timber across the hull every three feet or so is quite sufficient (Fig. 24). Though if your coach roof has a simple single curve it is easier to run 6″ × 1″ longitudinally between permanent or temporary bulkheads.

All the form work needs to be finished before you start putting on the foam.

Fig. 24. Temporary deck supports cut from 6″×1″.

On a catamaran it is possible to deck one hull and put one cabin side in place, then remove the form work, turn it inside out, and re-erect it in the other hull. This was the method I used. But I am sure it was a mistake. Although it would cost a bit more in timber to erect a full form work the saving in time and effort must make it well worth while in the end, especially if you use second-hand floor boarding.

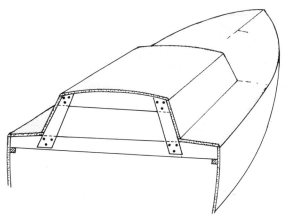

Fig. 25. The easiest type of superstructure in foam sandwich and the sort of foam work needed to support it.

Coach roofs that have a fairly hard angle between top and side are the quickest and easiest to make (Fig. 25). If you insist on having a generous radius, there is no reason why you should not have one. You will simply have to make up lengths of radius separately (Fig. 26). If the radius is only two or three inches you will find it easier to form the foam if you heat it first. A bath of very hot water is hot enough, or an electric fan heater can be used. Wrap the warm foam around a wooden or stout cardboard former (a core from the glass cloth perhaps). If you have the foam hot enough you will find it takes the curve of the former instantly and shows no tendency to spring back straight.

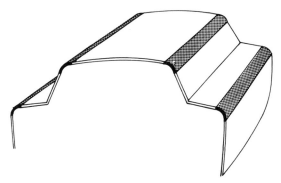

Fig. 26. If the section of your superstructure looks more like this, you will have to make up the shaded pieces as separate lengths.

Make sure that the foam is completely dry if you used water to heat it, then put resinglass on the inside of the curve. Use the same number of layers of glass as you use on the inside of the coach roof, but you will find it much easier to use chopped strand mat rather than woven roving.

Decks on the whole are rather large flat areas, so you will probably need a thicker foam than the one you used on the hull. We used 15 mm. foam on the decks, while the really large expanses of our cabin top and sides were made from foam 18 mm. thick.

When the form work is ready lay sheets of foam on it to make the decks, etc. Where you have to cut one piece of foam to fit another use a straight edge. This will save a lot of filling work later. You can use weights (polythene bags filled with sand perhaps) to hold the foam in place, but I used the odd nail through the foam into the form work. If you leave part of the nails sticking out they are easy to pull out with a pair of pincers.

At this stage the foam should be slightly oversize, say between half an inch and one inch all round except for the bottom of the cabin sides and front which want to be a reasonable fit with the deck. 'Reasonable fit' in this context means having gaps no bigger than about an inch or so. You will probably find it necessary to remove the cabin sides while you do the cabin top. If so, do not forget to allow for the thickness of the cabin sides when you cut the top. Tops for cabins that are almost straight-sided can of course be made from measurements, without actually putting the foam on to the form work.

Mark all the pieces of foam, preferably on the inside of the boat, across the joints so that the pieces can be matched up more or less exactly when the foam is on the ground.

You will now need a fairly flat wooden floor on which to lay out the foam and do the resinglass work. The foam does not all have to be laid out at the same time of course. There is no reason why the decks and other large pieces of foam should not be made in two or three pieces and joined together just before they are put on the hull. I made a perfectly satisfactory work area in the middle of a rough field (under the bridge deck of our catamaran to be precise). From three 8′ × 4′ sheets of plywood resting on scrap pieces of wood. Resin runs through the joints in the foam, so it helps if the 'floor' is covered with polythene.

Use the odd nail here and there to keep the foam in place on the floor. You will probably also find it necessary to use a few nails where the foam has a tendency to lift or curl at the edges. Leave part of the nails sticking out of the foam, then not only are they easy to pull out but you should find that you can work the woven roving of the first layer of glass down over the nail heads without any trouble and stretch it in the normal way.

It is a good idea to fill any large gaps between the pieces of foam with resin putty. But if you have covered your floor with polythene it is not necessary to touch the close-fitting joints. If you used a straight edge when you cut the foam, most of your joints should fit quite closely.

Pull the nails out after putting on the first layer of resinglass. Continue putting on resinglass until you have as many layers as your designer thinks you need. We had just two layers of 18 oz. unidirectional woven roving. Life will be easier when you come to fit the decks, etc., if you stop the resinglass about an inch from the edge of the foam, but it does not make a lot of difference.

Allow your last layer of resinglass to go off, then float resin over the whole piece to fill up the weave of the cloth. If you do this now you will not have the problem of working overhead once the decks are in place.

When this resin is hard take a Grinderette and scuff up all the areas that will be bonded to later, e.g. the edges, and bulk-head positions. This is another job that can be left until the decks are in place, but it is quicker and much, much easier to do it now.

It is a good idea to turn the piece over now and put two-inch-wide strips of chopped strand mat over all the joints in the foam. This is not strictly necessary on joints running across the hull, but unless you do it to joints running longitudinally they will open up as the foam is bent over the form work and you will have to do a lot of filling (Fig. 27).

Fig. 27.   Joints in foam with resinglass on one side only open up when the foam is bent. So it is a good idea to put some 2″ wide strips of mat on the other side.

The section is now ready for fitting. There is a possibility that the bond will break within the resinglass if you try to bend it too soon after laying up. So be patient, put the piece to one side for a day or two to cure, and carry on working on something else. In fact the best idea is to get all your deck- and coach-roof foam resinglassed on one side before you put any of it in position on the hull.

Start by putting the decks in place resinglass side down. Use weights to hold the foam to the camber of the form work. When the deck is snugly down on the form work go inside the hull and tack hull and deck together with small pieces of resinglass. Two-inch-square pieces of chopped strand mat every six inches or so should be adequate for this job, especially if you run a little resin along the joint as well. If for any reason you cannot get the deck foam to fit the form work with weights, you can screw blocks of wood to the inside of the hull just below the gunwale and then put screws up through these into the resinglass on the deck foam. If you do use blocks and screws in this way it will not be necessary to tack hull and deck together with resinglass.

Do not worry about the decks overhanging the hull a little. This can be sawn off later after the resinglass tacking pieces have had a chance to cure.

Hold the cabin sides in place with nails while you tack them in place with resinglass. Nails can be pushed up through the deck into the edges of the cabin sides and front, and the odd nail can be knocked through the cabin side into the bulkheads or form work. Again, put the resinglassed side inwards, though if you have dropped a clanger and glassed both the cabin sides on the same side of the foam it will not make much difference. Decks and cabin tops are normally symmetrical so you cannot resinglass them on the wrong side.

Fill any gaps between the cabin sides and front and decks with foam and resin putty. While this is going off you can trim the decks to size.

The easiest way I found to trim the decks was to stand on the deck and use an ordinary cross-cut wood saw to cut the foam and resinglass more or less flush with the hull. A pass with the Grinderette and the decks were completely flush with the hull sides. Another pass, very lightly this time, and the angle had been taken off the foam at the edge of the deck. The radius was completed by hand with coarse sandpaper on a flex sander (Fig. 28).

35. As this is only a small deck we used resin putty to glue it to the hull. Nails held it in place while the resin putty hardened. The U-shaped piece of resinglass on the right is to support the forward thwart.

105

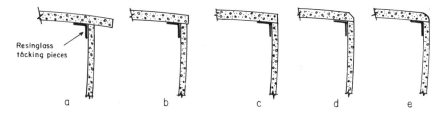

Fig. 28.   The stages in trimming the deck so that it is flush with the hull.

Return to the cabin sides and cut off the excess along the top.

Now comes the great moment when you put on the cabin roof. If it is a simple roof with only a single curve (like most) you can treat it in exactly the same way as you did the decks. If it is a more complicated affair, with some degree of double curvature, you will have to cut gussets out of the foam. It will probably be necessary to use screws up through the form work into the resinglass to pull the foam to shape. It is unlikely that

36.   The deck has been trimmed to size and the angle removed with the disc grinder.

106

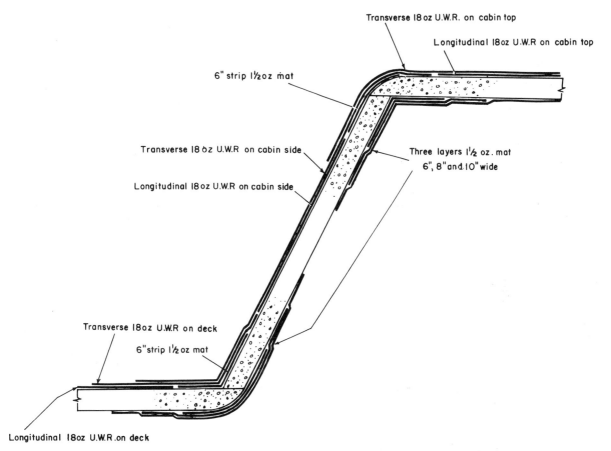

Transverse 18 oz U.W.R. on cabin top

Longitudinal 18oz U.W.R on cabin top

6" strip 1½oz mat

Three layers 1½ oz. mat
6", 8" and 10" wide

Transverse 18 oz U.W.R on cabin side

Longitudinal 18oz U.W.R on cabin side

Transverse 18oz U.W.R on deck

6"strip 1½oz mat

Longitudinal 18oz U.W.R.on deck

Fig. 29. Typical lay-up on cabin/deck joints to give maximum strength with minimum buildup of resinglass.

you will need to cut out more than two or three gussets, but the only way to find out is to try.

Fill any gaps in the structure with foam and resin putty and make sure there are no hard angles for the resinglass to go over.

The next job is to cut six-inch-wide strips of chopped strand mat to cover all the joints. The joints can be taped over with these strips before the main resinglass is put on the decks. It may be necessary to use the Grinderette on some of it if you cannot get the deck resinglass in place within twenty-four hours.

It is now just a question of putting the required thickness of resinglass over the cabin and decks. Just how you set about doing this will depend upon the design and how many layers of resinglass you are going to put on, Where possible it is a good idea to take the woven roving of the skin over any deck-cabin joints. This saves a bulky build up of extra layers of resinglass along the joints (Fig. 29).

37. The resinglass skin of the deck taken a little way down the hull to bond deck and hull together.

If your boat has flush decks the woven roving can be laid diagonally, all the layers being taken a little way down the hull to bond deck and hull together.

It is possible to lay the glass diagonally on a boat with a cabin, but in our case I thought this would complicate matters too much so I put the first layer of glass on longitudinally. The second layer was put on transversely and was run over the cabin-deck joints by four inches, and down the hull topsides by a similar amount. This covered every joint with three thicknesses of glass, except the deck-hull joint which had only one thickness each of chopped strand mat and woven roving. The deck-hull joint was completed with a ten-inch-wide strip of chopped strand mat (Fig. 30).

The superstructure is completed by putting resinglass over the joints on the inside of the boat to the required thickness. In our case we used three layers of chopped strand mat, six, eight and ten inches wide.

Most of the joints are overhead and it is a messy business brushing resin on to the deck heads and underside of the coach roof prior to positioning the strips of mat. We found it much cleaner, and quicker, to lay the strip of mat on a piece of formica or

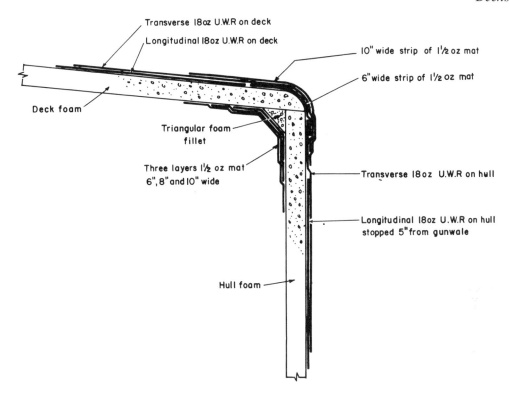

Fig. 30.   Typical lay-up at deck/hull joint.

plywood, brush resin on to it, then position it wet. Some of the pieces of mat done in this way needed a little resin dabbed on top; but most of it simply needed a good rolling, about ten minutes after it had been put up, and it was wetted out. Using this method it is necessary to work very quickly between starting to paint the resin on to the mat and getting the mat into place, otherwise the resin has time to penetrate the glass, dissolve the binders and instead of working with a strip of glass six inches wide and three feet long all you have is a sticky mess of resinglass.

Along the inside of our deck-hull joint we have a fillet for strength (Fig. 30). This was made from offcuts of 18 mm. foam. It seems daft now but I put off doing that job because I had not got a band saw on which to cut the foam. Of course once I made myself face up to the job it was quite straightforward to use a couple of pieces of wood as guides and cut the foam with an ordinary hand saw (Fig. 31). It did not take an hour to cut sufficient fillet foam for our hulls once I got started but I had been worrying about the job for weeks. There must be a moral there somewhere.

Once the fillets have been cut they can be stuck in place with blobs of resin putty, though of course any glue will do—it is not a structural joint. The strength is in the resinglass that goes on top of the fillet. We used Evostick when putting foam stringers

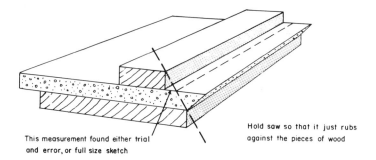

Hold saw so that it just rubs
against the pieces of wood

This measurement found either trial
and error, or full size sketch

Fig. 31. Simple method for cutting lengths of triangular section foam for the deck/hull joint. Two G-cramps hold everything firm during sawing, yet are quick and easy to re-position ready for the next piece.

in a conventional resinglass dinghy. Although expensive it was very convenient.

The decks can have resin floated over them to fill the weave of the cloth, while the cabin sides can be filled with resin putty.

Any conventional deck-cabin arrangement can be made using this method.

If the upper part of your design calls for lots of double, well-rounded curves, you may have to make the decks on a mould similar to the hull mould. To ensure a good fit between the decks and this mould it should be built on the finished hull.

If you should have any doubts about the ability of pre-resinglassed foam to follow the curves of your superstructure the best thing is to carry out a few experiments. Knock up three rough formers and mount them so that they look like a small part of the deck structure. Then see if a piece of foam resinglassed on one side will fit the formers. If the foam only needs a small cut here and there to make it fit properly all is well and you can proceed using the method outlined above.

If however you have to really cut the foam about to get anything like a fit, you will have to make a full mould for the superstructure and proceed as you did for the hull. It is virtually impossible to put up large areas of resinglass overhead like ceiling paper, so once the resinglass on the outside has cured the decks will have to be lifted off, turned over, and resinglassed on the inside.

Unless your design is considerably out of the ordinary, however, it is extremely unlikely that you will have to resort to making a mould for your superstructure.

Once the shell has been filled and sanded smooth it should be painted with two coats of two-pot polyurethane paint. Then of course the hull will need antifouling and deck paint put on in the normal way.

P.V.C. foam softens under heat and it is logical to paint the decks a light colour in order to reflect as much as possible, though Derek Kelsall assures me that boats of his have sailed around the West Indies for some time without any trouble of this nature.

110

Further uses of Foam and Resinglass

Foam sandwich can be used just about anywhere you would use plywood but for most fitting out purposes the extra cost is not justified. I think its use is justified in making curved components. We used it to make moulded seats for our cockpit, for instance. It also makes economic sense for the amateur to stick his offcuts of foam together and cover them with his offcuts of glass; this way he gets good strong panels suitable for cabin soles or bunk boards for the price of a few pounds of resin and a little labour.

It is possible to make masts from foam sandwich—the material cost is less than an

38. Polyurethane foam used as a former for a bow handle on the dinghy.

aluminium extrusion. Unfortunately not many have been made so there is very little data available, and it is still very much a case of 'suck it and see'.

While not foam sandwich in the strictest sense, low-density polyurethane foam can be used as a core material for many things, if it is covered with resinglass. Polyurethane foam is a reasonably cheap material and very easy to work; I used it for our centre boards and centre-board cases, but as with masts there is very little data available from which to work.

Offcuts of undirectional woven roving can be wrapped round 1″-diameter lengths of foam to make very cheap stanchions and pulpits. This is probably not worth doing if you have to buy glass and resin in small quantities especially for the job, but if you have just built a boat you will have lots of scraps of glass which are ideal, and resin is cheap in bulk.

To make our stanchions I laid out a strip of unidirectional woven roving about sixteen inches wide on a piece of waxed formica. This was then wetted out in the normal way, and while still wet it was wrapped round a piece of foam about one inch in diameter and slightly longer than the finished stanchion. It was hung up by a piece of string to dry, then finished with resin putty like the hull of the boat. The stanchions did not take very long to make and cost next to nothing.

We made oars and canoe paddles the same way, in fact we made a complete canoe on a polyurethane foam mould for less than half the price it would have cost us to buy a resinglass canoe in kit form.

Now we know how to use resinglass and have a supply of resin and offcuts of glass cloth it makes economic sense to use it almost everywhere, for things like boat hooks and boarding ladders, to say nothing of dinghies and canoes!

39. Our family testing the finished dinghy. The thwarts are a little too high, otherwise she is excellent, both under motor and oars.

Conclusion

John Beswick of Leen Valley Venture was absolutely right when he said foam sandwich building is as simple as it sounds. Probably the hardest job is convincing oneself that one is capable of making the mould. If you are capable of using a wood saw you can almost certainly make the mould.

We started resinglass work on our boat much too late in the year. If we ever make another boat we shall start on the mould in the autumn. This should not come to any harm under a polythene sheet for the winter. Once the mould is made measurements can be taken from it and the bulkheads, along with the deck form work, made in a garage somewhere. At the same time the foam for the decks and cabins can be cut roughly to shape and glassed on one side, in garage-sized pieces ready to be joined together just before going on the hull.

In the late spring the hull proper could be started. Estimate say three or four week-ends to get the foam on and faired up, then an early summer holiday to get the bulk of the resinglass work done, and a smallish mono-hull of thirty feet or so could be sailing by the end of the season.

But perhaps it is wise to heed Derek Kelsall's advice and not be too optimistic.

Equipment

For making the mould all you will need are a few basic wood-working tools, say a couple of saws, a hammer, try square, smallish plane, one or two chisels, a large pump screwdriver, a ten-foot steel tape, and an electric drill. Hire or borrow a portable jig saw for cutting the frames as these can all be done in a few hours if they are marked out ready.

Power tools are just about essential when you come to do resinglass work and if you are not within range of mains electricity you will have to fix up some sort of portable generating plant.

Power tools can be hired; in fact this is how we tried to operate, but it is not economical unless you can be absolutely sure that you will need the tool for only a given time and will then have no further use for it. Portable jig saws come into this category and so would a second Grinderette or finishing sander if you had a helper coming for just two or three weeks.

You will find it cheaper and much more convenient to buy outright a disc sander and a finishing sander before you start. The disc machine will be in constant use and both this tool and the finishing sander can earn their keep for many years at fitting-out time, even if you have to hire a generator to use them on the water.

A good disc sander is a most essential tool. Something has to be scuffed up or ground off on just about every working day. Initially we tried ordinary hand drills but they were much too slow. Then we tried a seven-inch angle grinder—this was fast enough but terribly heavy. Finally, when the boat was more or less built, we tried a Wolf Grinderette. This is a marvellous tool, light and fast, and I suggest you buy one before you start so that it is always to hand (it is good for shaping wood as well as resinglass). If there are going to be two or three of you working full time for a few weeks it would probably pay you to hire another just for that period. Or if two of you are working throughout the year making two boats you will probably find you save a lot of time by having two of these Grinderettes. As far as I know no other manufacturer makes anything like them.

A portable belt sander is quite good for scuffing up large areas but I am not sure it is much quicker than the Grinderette. If you live next door to the hire shop or already own a belt sander you can try it, but otherwise I suggest you stick to the disc machine.

When it comes to finishing, a decent-sized heavy-duty orbital sander is essential. We used a Wolf Sapphire $4\frac{1}{2}'' \times 9''$ machine, which proved to be excellent.

Having since used a good-quality disc sander and finishing sander I cannot understand how I prepared and painted a boat for so many years before without their aid.

Equipment for resinglass work need not be extensive and is quite cheap.

You will need some plastic buckets, say a dozen if there are two or three of you working together. We found the cheapest ones the best; they soon lost their handles, but they were so thin and flexible that hardened resin was easy to break out. As well as these we had three better-quality buckets with metal handles into which we weighed the resin.

A small spring balance which weighs up to 12 or 14 lb. is ideal for weighing the resin. Fishermen use them for the one that does not get away.

Automatic plastic dispensers for liquid catalyst are cheap and it is well worth having one. They come in two sizes, 10 cc. and 50 cc. For the quantities of resin used in building a boat the 50 cc. size is the one to get.

If you are using 500 lb. drums of resin, and this is far and away the cheapest method of buying, you will need a 2″ non-drip tap. Prices for these vary considerably but I can find no difference between the cheap and the expensive. We bought the cheapest and have no complaints.

Resin can be applied with mohair rollers, K. and C. Mouldings supply them, but we found them almost impossible to keep clean and so we started using cheap $1\frac{1}{2}″$ and 2″ brushes for all our resin work. No matter how careful you are eventually you will let your brushes go hard. There is nothing you can do with them then except throw them away. We tried a rather expensive, highly toxic solution sold as 'resin stripper' but as far as we could see its effect was negligible. Bearing this in mind the cheapest brushes you can find are the best; a dozen should see you through. We bought ours from K. and C. Mouldings.

When you come to use chopped strand mat you will need a washer roller. They come in different sizes and materials but there does not seem to be much to choose between them. We used 1″-diameter plastic rollers. Get two, one $3\frac{1}{2}″$ long and one 6″ long, and it is a good idea to get a spare set of washers for each while you are about it.

Scissors can be used to cut the glass, but a sharp knife is much quicker. We used two Stanley knives: one, which was kept reasonably clean, was used for cutting glass off the roll; the other, which was rapidly covered with a thick layer of resin and glass, was used for trimming wet resinglass. Not only is it expensive to keep putting new blades in these knives but it takes quite a lot of time; we found the best thing was to keep a fine oilstone handy and resharpen the blades from time to time, without taking them out of the knives.

Almost anything can be used for filling gaps with resin putty, but probably the best tools are an ordinary putty knife and a two-inch stripping knife. When you come to fairing up the outside of the hull you will need a metal plasterer's float.

We wore Martindale light fume respirators while sanding outside or inside and while doing resin work inside the finished boat. The pre-filters used in this mask, which we found no bother to wear by the way, quickly get clogged with glass dust and have to be replaced, so get a hundred when you buy the masks. The more expensive carbon filter should not get clogged for some time, if you use a pre-filter, but it is a good idea to have a spare for each mask. We had three masks and used about 150 pre-filters; towards the end all the carbon filters were clogged and had to be replaced.

Materials

P.V.C. FOAM

Rigid P.V.C. foam is probably the commonest core material used in the construction method we employed. Derek Kelsall uses Airex 01-18 of 5·29 lb.-per-cubic-foot density. This is manufactured in Switzerland and is imported by Impag Ltd.

When we were building our boat there was a supply problem on this material from the importers, so we got ours from Sandwich Marina. Airex has the great advantage for the amateur that it is flexible enough to form over a mould without heating.

'Plasticel' is an English, rigid P.V.C. foam manufactured by B.T.R. Industries Ltd. This foam was used in the construction of *Toria*, winner of the 1966 Round Britain Race. It is, however, quite rigid and has to be heated before it will bend.

A one-kilowatt electric fan heater blowing into a hardboard 'oven' generates sufficient heat for this, but for an amateur working more or less in the open I am not sure that this is a very practical proposition.

POLYURETHANE FOAM

Polyurethane foams are very brittle compared with Airex 01-18 and they do not bend very easily, even when heated. They are, however, very easy to work with a Surform and sandpaper and make very good core materials on which to put resinglass.

Polyurethane foam has better thermal-insulation properties than P.V.C. foam and it has to be heated to quite a high temperature before it distorts. I think it might be a good idea to make decks and superstructures from polyurethane rather than from P.V.C. foam, retaining the P.V.C. for the hull, where the flexibility and structural properties of the material can be used to advantage.

There are many suppliers of polyurethane foam; we dealt with Bulstrode Plastics and Chemical Co. Ltd. who are as cheap as anyone and gave good service.

POLYSTYRENE FOAM

This foam dissolves very readily in the styrene monomer in polyester resin, therefore it has no application in resinglass work, unless it is first treated with a protective coating —which all seems a bit of a bother to me when polyurethane is available. It can be used in block form as buoyancy, but as polyurethane foam has a lower rate of water absorption it is to be preferred in this application, even though it is about four times the price.

GLASS

Chopped strand mat is rated at so many ounces per square foot and for the job it has to do in a sandwich craft, $1\frac{1}{2}$ oz. mat is the most convenient to use. Woven cloths on the other hand are rated at so many ounces per square yard which I found all very confusing at first but now I have learned to live with it.

Glass cloth and mat for marine use should be made from 'E' glass. And it is not worth buying glass from a dubious source unless it is in an obvioulsy unopened carton which states quite clearly that it is of 'E' standard.

Chopped strand mat has very little place in foam sandwich boats because of its relatively poor strength–weight characteristics compared with woven cloths. Some however is necessary. We used 'Dee' glass simply because that is what we were sent and we also used some Swedish mat from E. R. Birch.

The 'Dee' glass was very stiff with binders and it took a long time for the resin to soak through. The Swedish glass was soft and formed readily and it seemed to wet out more easily, but it frayed at the edges and disintegrated if we tried to move it once the resin was on.

For the job we were doing I would have liked a mat somewhere between the two. But it is not terribly important, provided it is 'E' glass; go for the cheapest available and adopt a method of working to suit the glass.

Woven roving is used where good strength–weight characteristics are required and the extra time needed to wet out the cloth compared with the mat is of little importance. Normal woven roving, in which the rovings run in two directions, has to be overlapped at the edges just like mat and this gives problems in finishing the outside of a sandwich boat.

Unidirectional woven roving, in which the rovings run all one way, can however be laid so that the edges are butt-joined. A resinglass skin can then be built up, layer on layer, with the cloth running first one way then the other, like plywood.

When using unidirectional woven roving it is easiest if you think in terms of wood and ask yourself, 'Which way should the grain run for maximum strength?'. Then it is a simple matter to make a resinglass lay up in which the glass rovings follow the ideal path.

There are a number of manufacturers of unidirectional glass cloths but, along with Sandwich Marina, we used Marglass 280 which is an 18 oz. unidirectional woven roving, and comes in rolls 4' wide.

RESIN

We used a general-purpose polyester resin from Strand Glass Ltd. This resin was rather thick, however, and it needed nearly 2 lb. of resin to wet out each pound of woven roving. A thin marine resin would have been better and such a resin should wet out easily at a ration of 1 to $1\frac{1}{2}$ lb. of resin to each pound of glass.

Because marine resin is so thin it will readily drain down the sides of the hull. This is not very important on the outside—you will just waste a lot of resin if you use too much—on the inside it will form a resin puddle in the bottom of the hull, which is not a good thing. Styrene Monomer is used to thin resin. It also has a softening effect on P.V.C. foam and resin with a styrene content of more than 40 per cent should not be used. But see Derek Kelsall's comment on page 61.

Prices of resin vary considerably from supplier to supplier, so it is a good idea to shop around. Resin is very expensive in small lots and it pays handsomely to buy in 500 lb. drums if you can. Using a lever, and possibly a jack, you should have no difficulty handling a 500 lb. drum of resin.

While some moulders store their resin outside, ideally it should have some sort of cover to protect it from the sun. A piece of hardboard on a light frame would be quite adequate for an amateur with two or three drums only. It is as well to roll a new drum of resin around for a few minutes before you put the tap in, to make sure it is well mixed up.

CATALYST

Catalyst is expensive so check whether it is included in the price quoted for the resin. Liquid catalyst is easier to measure than the paste one but make sure it is well mixed into the resin.

If you are expecting to have to do resin work when the temperature is low tell your resin supplier so he can advise on the quantity of catalyst you will need. Our resin was a general sort of one and we used on average $3\frac{1}{2}$ cc. of catalyst for each pound of resin (450 cc. catalyst = 1 lb.).

ACCELERATOR

This should have been added by the resin supplier and need not concern you—unless you are working at very low temperatures when you may have to add some more.

TIMBER

Again prices vary enormously and it pays to buy as high up the chain of supply as you can.

All the timber for our mould was secondhand, and cost half the price of new. We found the supplier by looking in the small ads in the local paper.

To get our marine ply we 'phoned around half a dozen local suppliers and ordered from the cheapest.

FILLER

Filler is cheap, but it is expensive to transport, so it helps if you can buy locally and collect yourself or buy it when you order a lot of other stuff and get the supplier to pay the carriage.

We used a couple of bags of a French filler known as B.L.H., which was quite all right for general filling of foam and that sort of thing. But it is very hard, too hard in fact, for filling the outside of a boat, except a very small one which is going to get a lot of hard wear, like a dinghy. One pound of B.L.H. with $\frac{1}{3}$ lb. of resin will fill about three square feet of boat, which makes it rather heavy.

The bulk of the filling should be done with the cheapest talc filler, this will be easier to work than the hard fillers, yet still hard enough for the job it has to do. We used Talc 16092 from Lonabarc Ltd., and Garotalc 132 from K. and C. Mouldings; one pound of these with $\frac{2}{3}$ lb. of resin should cover about six square feet of boat surface.

ABRASIVES

Start with three grades of disc for the Grinderette. To see how things go I suggest you buy six each of 16 grit, 36 grit, and 80 grit. Get fibre-backed aluminium oxide discs; paper discs do not last five minutes. Use the 16-grit discs on resin that has recently gone off; the 36-grit discs on cured resin; and the 80-grit discs on hard resin where you want a reasonable finish.

If you have to scuff up a large area of resinglass that is over twenty-four hours' old use 36-grit discs, or 36-grit belts in a portable belt sander.

For use with the orbital sander get a roll of 40-grit aluminium oxide paper for initial sanding and one of 140 grit for final smoothing. You may need more eventually but just get one of each initially to see how things go.

ACETONE

Is essential for cleaning brushes and tools, start off with about five gallons. Acetone is expensive if you buy it from a chemist, and difficult to find elsewhere, so start looking for a cheap source of supply early in your planning stage. Probably the best place to start looking is at a local resinglass-moulding works. We obtained ours from E. R. Birch.

BARRIER CREAM/HAND CREAM

Kerodex and Kerocleanse are used by the professional moulders, and we found them very good. But the Kerocleanse was inclined to sting. We used 14 lb. of each, but on a smaller boat you would probably get by with half this quantity.

Suppliers

Prices vary considerably from supplier to supplier for identical products, so you can save a lot of money by shopping round. Some suppliers pay the cost of transport on orders over a certain value, others expect the customer to foot the entire bill no matter how large the order. This is worth bearing in mind when working out which is the cheapest source. We spent over £25 in carriage charges of one sort and another, enough to have bought us another disc sander if only we had been more awake.

Buying in fairly large quantities we found many suppliers were prepared to give us a discount, provided we asked for it. A penny a pound off the price of resin when you are buying 3,000 lb. comes to a worthwhile amount of cash.

The following list of suppliers is not meant to be exhaustive. It is a list of the people we dealt with, which means that they are as competitive as anyone I could find and they gave good service. Conditions change, however, and it is quite possible that you can find more competitive prices nearer home. Certainly pay a visit to any smallish moulding works in your area. You may find one prepared to supply you with most of your requirements at little more than the cost to him.

I am afraid I can offer no help in the matter of suppliers to builders in America, Australia, New Zealand, or anywhere else outside Britain. But I have told you what you will need, which is over half the battle and a few letters or 'phone calls should soon turn up people ready to sell the stuff to you.

Frederick Attwood Ltd.,
Forest Works,
Arterial Road,
Rayleigh,
Essex.

Southend 523444

Crane hire people, extremely efficient.

B.T.R. Industries Ltd.,
Thameside Industrial Estate,
Silvertown, London,
E.16.

Manufacturers and suppliers of Plasticell rigid P.V.C. foam.

Basin Yacht Stores, Heybridge Basin, Maldon, Essex.	Hullbridge Yacht Stores, 265, Ferry Road, Hullbridge, Essex.

General chandlery, glue and fastenings, prepared to give a discount on bulk purchases. Common hard woods at reasonable prices.

E. R. Birch,   Canvey Island 4040
Unit 3, Mulberry Road,
Canvey Island,
Essex.

Moulders primarily, but happy to supply any of the materials they use, e.g. marine resin, mat, acetone. Competitive prices but carriage extra.

Bulstrode Plastics and Chemical Co. Ltd.   01–855 6806
Bulstrode House,
Bowater Road,
Woolwich, London,
S.E.16.

Polyurethane foam and ingredients for making your own polyurethane foam.

John S. Craig & Co. Ltd.,   Govan 77791
12–40 Bogmoor Road,
Glasgow,
S.W.1.

Manufacturers and suppliers of two-part polyurethane paint, anti-fouling, etc. Gallon packs are their smallest size but excellent paint (good enough for the Q.E.2) and cheaper than most.

Impag (London) Ltd.,   01–480 5964
61/62 Crutched Friars.
London,
E.C.3.

Importers of Airex rigid P.V.C. foam. To be sure of supply, check early in planning stage.

126

K. & C. Mouldings (England) Ltd.,   Diss 2660
Spa House,
Shelfanger, Diss,
Norfolk.

Suppliers of all materials and equipment used in resinglass work, carriage extra.

Derek Kelsall,   Sandwich 3335
Sandwich Marina,
Sandwich,
Kent.

Designer of multi-hulls, prepared to advise on all aspects of foam sandwich construction. Fees reasonable, but it is unfair to expect him to spend time and effort on your problems without some sort of payment.

Lonabarc. Ltd.,   01–554 6461
253, Cranbrook Road,
Ilford,
Essex.

Talc 16092 filler. Transportation is of course likely to be expensive if you live very far away.

Marglass Ltd.,
Sherbourne,
Dorset.

Manufacturers of Marglass 280, 18 oz. unidirectional woven roving. To be sure of supply, check early.

A. V. Rogers & Son,   Southend on Sea
58, East Street,   63166
Prittlewell,
Essex.

Cheap imported marine plywood to B.S. 1088.

A.J.S. Sandwich Yacht Construction Co. Ltd., Sandwich 3335
Sandwich Marina,
Sandwich,
Kent.

Builders in foam sandwich. Prepared to supply materials.

Strand Glass Co. Ltd.,   01–560 0978
Brentway Trading Estate,
Brentford,
Middlesex.

Suppliers of all materials and equipment used in resinglass work. No carriage charges on orders over £40.

Wolf Electric Tools Ltd.,   01–998 2911
Head Office,
Pioneer Works,
Hanger Lane, London,
W.5.

Manufacturers of the Wolf Grinderette and Sapphire finishing sander. Do not supply direct, but will give you the address of your nearest agent if you cannot find him.

Screws, abrasives, masking tape, etc., we bought from local tool shops; prices seem to be fairly standard.